USING THE JESUS PRAYER

Published by
The Bible Reading Fellowship
15 The Chambers, Vineyard
Abingdon OX14 3FE
United Kingdom
Tel: +44 (0)1865 319700
Email: enquiries@brf.org.uk
Website: www.brf.org.uk
BRF is a Registered Charity

ISBN 978 1 84101 778 5

First published 2014

10 9 8 7 6 5 4 3 2 1 0

Acknowledgements
Unless otherwise stated, scripture quotations are taken from the New Revised Standard Version of the Bible, Anglicised edition, copyright © 1989, 1995 by the Division of Christian Education of the National Council of the Churches of Christ in the United States of America, and are used by permission. All rights reserved.

Scripture quotations taken from The Holy Bible, New International Version (Anglicised edition) copyright © 1979, 1984, 2011 by Biblica. Used by permission of Hodder & Stoughton Publishers, an Hachette UK company. All rights reserved. 'NIV' is a registered trademark of Biblica. UK trademark number 1448790.

Cover photo: © Heather Knight

A catalogue record for this book is available from the British Library

Printed and bound by CPI Group (UK) Ltd, Croydon CR0 4YY

USING THE JESUS PRAYER

STEPS TO A SIMPLER CHRISTIAN LIFE

JOHN TWISLETON

Contents

Foreword

The recurring word in John Twisleton's attractive introduction to the Jesus Prayer is 'simple'. In a culture that demands of us so much choice and such a rapid pace of change, the offer of something simple is extremely welcome, and this is particularly true in the case of exploring faith in Jesus Christ and the experience of prayer.

The vast majority of people in Britain today have little or no direct experience of Christianity, but we are increasingly aware of living in a multiracial society in which the practice of religion is an integral part of the life of Muslims, Jews, Hindus and Sikhs. Their practice of prayer and worship is a core element of religious education in our schools, raising the question of what prayer is and how it is done.

The question of prayer is also raised for us in other circumstances of our personal and national life. At moments of bereavement and of celebration we look for the words and actions of prayer that can adequately express our most profound emotions.

The Jesus Prayer presents us with an experience of Christian prayer that enfolds, and is greater than, the preoccupations and fashions of our own day. It invites us into a rhythm of encounter with God that has been made smooth by centuries of use. Its simplicity transcends the barriers of language and culture, and is attuned to the spirituality of a person of any age or capacity.

As a pastor and theologian, John Twisleton has been

prompted to make available for us this example of Christian prayer as one that's well suited to the needs of our time. Simplicity is the door to an immediate and authentic experience of the God whom Christians seek to know more fully. In a 24/7 age that never rests, this is an any-time, any-place prayer for any person.

+Martin Cicestr

Introduction

'I've found it!' Archimedes is supposed to have shouted—'Eureka!'—as he jumped out of the bath with the solution to the king's challenge to find out whether his gold crown was adulterated by silver. In the bath, Archimedes had noticed water flowing out as his body sank down, and concluded that the volume of water displaced equalled the volume of his body immersed in the water. This meant that he'd found a way to measure the density of the crown and compare it with a bar of pure gold.

My own 'eureka moments' have been few and far between but they've defined and simplified my life. This book flows from one of them—the discovery of the Jesus Prayer of Eastern Orthodox Christianity. It was a less dramatic 'eureka' than my call to priesthood or marriage to my wife Anne, since I'd been aware of the Jesus Prayer for 30 years before it surfaced as the simplification to Christian life that I now find it to be. Nevertheless I feel impelled to write of it as the simplifier it has become to me and could become to you.

I have come to believe that there is nothing new in Christianity, just the need to enter the day-by-day newness of Jesus. In the following pages I look at how that newness has refreshed me through reciting 'Lord Jesus Christ, Son of God, have mercy on me, a sinner' so as to realise in my life the biblical injunction to pray at all times. The Jesus Prayer is inhabited by Jesus, who is an effective reminder that God is love and has mercy on us frail mortals. It is a prayer discipline that states the simple good news of Christianity, provides Holy Spirit empowerment to bypass distracted minds, links worship with life, and resonates with the faith and prayer of the church through the ages.

The book starts by reflecting on the good news intrinsic to the Jesus Prayer. It goes on to show how the spiritual discipline of continuously saying it, which is found in Orthodox Christianity, builds from its biblical base. We then change gear to look at how the simplification of anxiety and mental distraction that many people seek in Buddhist-type 'mindfulness' exercises can be found in the Jesus Prayer as a 'God-given mantra'. *Using the Jesus Prayer* concludes with practical advice about saying the Jesus Prayer and about how it helps in relating worship to life and in building up the integrity of Christian believers.

Archimedes helped the king purify his gold through his 'eureka moment'. I believe the Jesus Prayer to be a gift and task accomplishing spiritual purification. Its growing use is part of the Holy Spirit's unpacking in our day of the solid riches of Orthodoxy, to help ground the more fluid Catholic and Reformed traditions that often struggle to stand their ground and make disciples.

As an Anglican, I am grateful for Catholic, Reformed and Orthodox traditions, in all of which I trace the golden thread of devotion to the name of Jesus. It is that devotion I would like to commend through invitation to welcome the gift and task of the Jesus Prayer.

> ***The sun, passing over the earth, produces daylight; the holy and worshipful Name of the Lord Jesus, constantly shining in the mind, produces a measureless number of sun-like thoughts.***
>
> HESYCHIUS OF JERUSALEM[1]

CHAPTER 1

A simple discovery

Lord Jesus Christ, Son of God

Say to yourself very often about everything that happens, 'God loves me! What joy!' And reply boldly, 'And I truly love him too!' then go quite simply about all that you have to do and do not philosophise any more. For these two phrases are beyond all thought and do more for us than any thought could do; they are all sufficing.[2]

That advice from Abbé Henri de Tourville (1842–1903) gives a simple summary of the Christian religion: no need to philosophise, just dwell in God's love and go about all that you have to do, for this truth beyond all thought is all sufficing. I have spent my life calling myself and others back again and again to that advice.

I write mindful of Colin, who died in good heart this morning after such a reminder through confession, anointing and Eucharist. As priest in a country parish, my whole ministry is one of reminder, not least to myself, that 'God so loved the world that he gave his only Son, so that everyone who believes in him may not perish but may have eternal life' (John 3:16). It is that reality that surrounds us from cradle to grave, and only by keeping alert to it can we live to the full. As Colin accepted absolution and communion, I was in no doubt that he was embracing through these sacraments the love of the one we cannot see, into whose presence he passed shortly afterwards. I was privileged to witness a final surrender, acting out those words of de Tourville: 'God loves me! What joy! And I truly love him too!' Christianity's so simple—even if holding ourselves to it can be far from simple because of God's invisibility and the things we suffer that could be read as pointing against the reality of his love.

I sped to Colin's house this morning from my prayers, which now include 30 minutes' recitation of the Jesus Prayer: 'Lord Jesus Christ, Son of God, have mercy on me, a sinner.' That prayer still echoes within me as I sit down at the computer to start this book. Indeed, I would not be writing unless that prayer were always with me, holding me to God's love with all of my heart, as the discovery it has continued to be over the last six years of my life. As Bishop Kallistos Ware writes:

> *Part of the distinctive value of the Jesus Prayer lies precisely in the fact that, because of its radical simplicity, it can be prayed in conditions of distraction when more complex forms of prayer are impossible. It is especially helpful in moments of tension and grave anxiety. The 'free' use of the Jesus Prayer enables us to bridge the gap between our explicit 'times of prayer'—whether at church services or alone in our own room—and the normal activities of daily life.*[3]

I had known of the Jesus Prayer for 30 years before I welcomed it as a gift and a task to help us 'pray without ceasing' (1 Thessalonians 5:17). When I first heard of it, I had experienced renewal in the Holy Spirit, as I have described in my earlier book, *Meet Jesus*.[4] The capacity for praying in tongues to help us 'pray in the Spirit at all times' (Ephesians 6:18) is familiar to me, and over the years I have related this gift to the teaching and practice of the church through the ages, not least to that of the Orthodox anthology known as *The Philokalia*, which advises on prayer of the heart.[5] Both the Jesus Prayer and prayer in tongues serve to bypass mental distraction and help to simplify Christian life and devotion, and later on in this book I will be returning to the way they can relate to the enrichment of both practices. As a priest leading worship, attending to people's joys and sorrows and the stresses and strains of church administration, I have found the Jesus Prayer an invaluable aid. This is because of the simple message it holds before me that God loves me and all that is, minute by minute, day by day and for all eternity.

In this chapter and the next, I want to examine the biblical construction of the two parts of the Jesus Prayer before moving on to draw wisdom from its use throughout the Christian centuries, to see how it helps relate worship to life and build the integrity of Christian believers.

GOD LOVES US

As I prepared Colin to go to God in old age and infirmity, it seemed to me that these words of the apostle Paul had a particular resonance: 'If the Spirit of him who raised Jesus from the dead dwells in you, he who raised Christ from the dead will give life to your mortal bodies also through his Spirit that dwells in you' (Romans 8:11). Though his mortal body was fast deteriorating, Colin's inner life was well fortified, so I imagined his passing as being a journey into a new realm where that life would burst into a further blossoming at our prayer. God who'd given Colin life had also given him *his own life*. In welcoming that eternal life in word and sacrament into ourselves, as Colin did, throughout our earthly lifetime, our 'inside selves' or souls are made capable of immortality. Almost my last words to Colin were 'The body of Our Lord Jesus Christ which was shed for thee preserve thy body and soul unto everlasting life.'[6] These words left him, by his own admittance, in good heart and ready to pass to the unveiled love of God.

O God, unseen yet ever near, thy presence may we feel;
and thus inspired with holy fear, before thine altar kneel.

We come, obedient to thy word, to feast on heav'nly food;
our meat the body of the Lord, our drink his precious blood.

Thus may we all thy word obey, for we, O God, are thine;
and go rejoicing on our way, renewed with strength divine.[7]

Edward Osler's Communion hymn captures the obedience and empowerment of the Eucharist, that greatest sacrament or sign of God's love, bringing us his life, making us more fully his, strengthening us to 'go rejoicing on our way' through life and death.

God loves us: he is 'unseen but ever near'. Just as the air around is invisible but is known when the wind blows, so the love of God announces itself in a prayer, a word of scripture or a sip of wine. Above all, that love shows itself in the birth, life, death and resurrection of Jesus Christ, Son of God, who is the sign above all signs that scripture points to and the sacraments reveal.

People sometimes complain at the idea of a loving God. They read signs of futility and decay in the world around them rather than the goodness, beauty and truth that reflect the Creator. It is one of the mysteries of life that some are blinded to a loving God, while others are impatient with unbelievers, like Paul, who wrote, 'Ever since the creation of the world his eternal power and divine nature, invisible though they are, have been understood and seen through the things he has made. So they are without excuse' (Romans 1:20). When you catch sight of the love of God, it's as if the world lights up with his glory and even the dark spaces gain meaning. The supreme sign of his love is that he did not keep himself aloof from our dark spaces but, rather, came to enter them and die as one of us. The eye of faith recognises that it can therefore never be said of the God and Father of Jesus that he expects anything of us that he is not prepared to go through himself. As Isaiah's 'Song of the Lord's Gracious Deeds', read at Anglican Evening Prayer in Passiontide, expresses it:

Who is this that comes from Edom,
coming from Bozrah, his garments stained crimson?

Who is this in glorious apparel,
marching in the greatness of his strength?

'It is I, who announce that right has won the day,
it is I' says the Lord, 'for I am mighty to save.'

'Why are your robes all red, O Lord,
and your garments like theirs who tread the winepress?'

'I have trodden the winepress alone,
and from the peoples no one was with me.'

I will recount the gracious deeds of the Lord,
the praises of the Most High;

all that God has done for us in his mercy,
by his many acts of love.

For God said, 'Surely, they are my people,
my children who will not deal falsely,'
and he became their Saviour in all their distress.

So God redeemed them by his love and pity;
He lifted them up and carried them
through all the days of old.

ISAIAH 63:1–3A, 7–9[8]

That awesome picture of the Saviour in crimson garments, treading the winepress, was composed centuries before Jesus suffered. Just as creation opens up God's glory to the eye of faith, so the Old Testament prophet Isaiah informs the same eye of faith about the immensity of God's love that acts on our behalf with love and pity, to redeem us from our sins and carry us forward into his possibilities. By his death and resurrection, Jesus Christ is revealed as the greatest sign of God's love, foretold by the biblical prophets, present in the church's preaching and sacraments and destined to bring all things together.

In the early years of persecution, when a Christian met a stranger on the road, he sometimes drew one arc of a simple fish outline in the dirt. If the stranger drew the other arc, both believers knew they were in safe company. The early

Christians used the secret sign of the fish because the Greek word for fish, *ichthus*, was an acronym for 'Jesus Christ, Son of God and Saviour', the earliest creed and the shortest statement of Christian faith. The Jesus Prayer is a short expansion of that personal creed, which is expressed by Paul, for example, when he says, 'I live by faith in the Son of God, who loved me and gave himself for me' (Galatians 2:20b).

'Lord Jesus Christ, Son of God' implies that the historical figure of Jesus is the universal Lord and Son of God. Behind that statement is the implication that the invisible God has, in one human life at one time and place, made himself visible, supremely upon the cross, showing us his love to be witnessed to every generation. God who made all and loves all desires to claim all, starting with the human race made in his image. The first clause of the Jesus Prayer affirms the good news that Jesus brings to our lives, news that we come from God, we belong to God and we go to God. 'The eternal God is your refuge, and underneath are the everlasting arms' (Deuteronomy 33:27, NIV).

'How happy God is in loving us!' writes Abbé de Tourville. 'Like parents who adore their children. It is really just like that and it is *grand*, and just what we should expect of God. It is also necessary for us, poor little creatures that we are. Praise God!'[9]

THE NAME OF JESUS

The Hebrews of the Old Testament saw the names given to people and things not as a sort of 'add-on' but as their basic constituent. Several stories, like that of Jacob and the angel (Genesis 32:29), show a resistance to revealing names, since that knowledge would give the enquirer control over the one in question. The name of God is particularly opaque and awesome, as is indicated in the conversation recorded in Exodus between Moses and God:

> *Moses said to God, 'If I come to the Israelites and say to them, "The God of your ancestors has sent me to you," and they ask me, "What is his name?" what shall I say to them?' God said to Moses, 'I am who I am.' He said further, 'Thus you shall say to the Israelites, "I am has sent me to you."'* **(Exodus 3:13–14)**

This reticence makes his revelation as the God and Father of Jesus Christ quite extraordinary. 'I am who I am' could be interpreted as 'I will be who I will be.' God is above any being since he is the ground of all being. The idea that God would take a human name was and is offensive to the Jewish people, as well as to Muslims. That offence, true to the spirit of Exodus 3, is shown in this Gospel altercation, where Jesus is reported as identifying himself with God's majestic 'I am': 'Jesus said to [the Jews], "Very truly, I tell you, before Abraham was, I am." So they picked up stones to throw at him' (John 8:58–59a).

In Christian understanding, the revelation of God to Moses is not contradicted but is deepened by God's coming to walk upon earth in the person of Jesus Christ. The choice of the name 'Jesus' hints at his succession to Moses, since it is the Greek form of 'Joshua', the name of Moses' successor as Israel's leader, meaning 'God saves'. This understanding of Jesus' coming, life, death and resurrection as having saving significance for us all is there throughout the New Testament. For example, Matthew records an angel appearing to settle Joseph's anxiety about Mary's unexpected pregnancy and saying, 'The child conceived in her is from the Holy Spirit.

She will bear a son, and you are to name him Jesus, for he will save his people from their sins' (Matthew 1:20b–21).

Repetition of the name of Jesus has unique spiritual power. Here is 'the name that is above every name' because God 'highly exalted' Jesus (Philippians 2:9). If using any name brings a particular person to mind, how much more the name of the one offered in sacrifice for our sins and exalted in his resurrection and ascension to heaven? If God is in all things, how much will he be in the name he chose to bear as our Saviour, of whom scripture says, 'There is salvation in no one else, for there is no other name under heaven given among mortals by which we must be saved' (Acts 4:12)? Even before his crucifixion, Jesus' disciples ministered healing and deliverance in their master's name, as recorded in the return of the 70 he commissioned for that purpose: 'The seventy returned with joy, saying, "Lord, in your name even the demons submit to us!"' (Luke 10:17).

The phrase 'Lord Jesus Christ, Son of God' is first used by Peter at the centre and turning point of Matthew's Gospel:

> *Now when Jesus came into the district of Caesarea Philippi, he asked his disciples, 'Who do people say that the Son of Man is?' And they said, 'Some say John the Baptist, but others Elijah, and still others Jeremiah or one of the prophets.' He said to them, 'But who do you say that I am?' Simon Peter answered, 'You are the Messiah, the Son of the living God.' And Jesus answered him, 'Blessed are you, Simon son of Jonah! For flesh and blood has not revealed this to you, but my Father in heaven.'* (Matthew 16:13–17)

Peter, the very first to name Jesus as Son of God, is empowered at Pentecost to minister in that name. After invoking the name of Jesus over a lame man, he sees the man healed and 'walking and leaping and praising God' (Acts 3:8b), an image of freedom in the Spirit that captures for ages to come the spiritual power in the name of Jesus.

When I recite the Jesus Prayer, I am aware of the power that lies in the name of Jesus, especially as it engages with my base thoughts and desires. The prayer helps us achieve the aspiration of Colossians 3:17: 'Whatever you do, in word or deed, do everything in the name of the Lord Jesus, giving thanks to God the Father through him.' The continuous recitation of the Jesus Prayer is a counter to all the base aspirations in me. It is a form of spiritual warfare, as vividly described by the sixth-century Saint John of the Ladder, who makes this injunction: 'Flog the foes with the name of Jesus; for there is no stronger weapon against them either in heaven or on earth.'[10]

The power there is in reciting the holy name in the Jesus Prayer is nothing magical but, as scripture indicates, is linked to trusting the word of God and the Holy Spirit. We take Jesus at his word when he says, 'Very truly, I tell you, if you ask anything of the Father in my name, he will give it to you' (John 16:23), mindful that 'no one can say "Jesus is Lord" except by the Holy Spirit' (1 Corinthians 12:3). It is the power of the truth, no less, since Christian prayer is inseparable from Christian belief, at the centre of which lies the divinity of Christ. To pray 'Lord Jesus Christ, Son of God...' is to affirm something revealed from God, nothing we could ourselves make up, and the joyful freedom associated with this prayer is the fruit of Christ's promise: 'If you continue in my word, you are truly my disciples; and you will know the truth, and the truth will make you free' (John 8:31–32).

A SIMPLE DISCOVERY

'Lord Jesus Christ, Son of God, have mercy on me, a sinner,' I repeated on the rowing machine. Time in the gym helps get me out of my mind into my body, and that was especially welcome as I have lacked exercise today. I have been sitting around—at prayer, with the family or the computer, the school head, a bereaved family, home communicants and a troubled parent, as well as putting my mind to celebrating the Eucharist, burying cremated remains and finishing the weekly news sheet. Gym time helps our bodily well-being. It can also be deep thinking time, though this can turn into anxious mental preoccupation, which is why I think many people wear headphones to engage their minds as they exercise their bodies. No headphones today, I thought, but a conscious coming back into the Lord's presence. The Jesus Prayer took something of an act of will at first (though it does flow on unconsciously, as I will explain later) but the holy name of Jesus began to centre and simplify my being. My accent today was on the first phrase, 'Lord Jesus Christ, Son of God', as I repeated the prayer and allowed the name of Jesus to open me to the love of God, which casts out anxiety and useless preoccupation.

There are many ways of praying, and the Jesus Prayer is but one. Over the years, I have moved between reading set prayers, silent attention, singing hymns or choruses, praying or singing in the Spirit to complement the divine offices of morning, midday, evening and night prayer, which are the staple of a priest. As I have welcomed the Jesus Prayer, it has not been to the exclusion of these forms or of the day-by-day Eucharist, but as a gift and task that flows between them and into my relationships, work and recreation. As I recovered this prayer in the gym, it flowed with the rowing movement, just as its phrasing fits with the natural rhythm of breathing in and out (as I shall explain later). As the prayer centred me, I became aware again of God's love present alongside me in Jesus, of a dispelling of negative preoccupation and an outward focus upon all those exercising around me. The Lord used my recovered discipline of continuous recitation to turn me out of myself in loving intercession towards my neighbours. This was expressed later, in some friendly greetings and one conversation with a young man who was intrigued about why some of his friends had started attending a neighbouring church that was full of young people.

'God-incidences' such as these often follow prayer of whatever kind. A standard definition of prayer is that it 'raises heart and mind to God'. In doing so, it lifts us from self-preoccupation into God's preoccupation, placing us in situations where we feel we are very much in the right time and place. This is the discovery I need day by day, hour by hour, wherever I am—at the gym or at church—the repeated discovery that I am living in the love of God.

This simple discovery is at the heart of Christian motivation. As Bishop Kallistos writes:

> *Concentrate your whole self, all your ardour and devotion, upon the person of the Saviour. Feel his presence. Speak to him with love. If your attention wanders, as undoubtedly it will, do not be discouraged; gently, without exasperation or inner anger, bring it back. If it wanders again and again, then again and yet again bring it back. Return to the centre—to the living and personal centre, Jesus Christ. Look on the Invocation not so much as prayer emptied of thoughts, but as prayer filled with the Beloved.*

Let it be, in the richest sense of the word, a prayer of affection—*although not of a self-induced emotional excitement. For while the Jesus Prayer is certainly far more than 'affective' prayer in the technical Western sense, it is with our loving affection that we do right to begin.*[11]

CHAPTER 2

A simple choice

Have mercy on me, a sinner

It's lambing season and we are all aware of this in the village. As I look out of the Rectory, the young lambs are running joyfully in the field below. They are an uplifting image of freedom that touches a spring inside me. Their excitement at life is evident as they go leaping and bounding around. They are blissfully unaware of the commercial aspect of their life and of its brevity. In this moment they are an image of joyful abandonment that refreshes my spirit. Their seeming carelessness disappears, however, as soon as their mothers lift themselves from the ground: they dart underneath for milk, driven, as all animals are, including myself, by the need for food. As I watch them I am uplifted, and as I am lifted I become aware of how unlike a carefree lamb's my life is today. I am regretful of past faults, mindful of a load of administration pressing upon me and somewhat anxious about finding new volunteers to fill vacancies that have recently appeared among church officers.

'Lord Jesus Christ, Son of God.' I repeat the Jesus Prayer under my breath and find myself emphasising today the second phrase: 'have mercy on me, a sinner'. Unlike the lambs, I am aware of the weight of care that pulls my spirit down. For them each moment stands alone, with no past regrets or future anxieties—indeed, no real sense of past or future accomplishment. They prosper without repentance, just following the law of nature, since they are incapable of the disobedience that is mine. Their capacity to skip down the field shows a mastery over gravity that, while warming my heart, challenges my sinful weight of self-preoccupation. In repeating the Jesus Prayer, I make a choice for that to be lifted from me, 'laying aside every weight and the sin that clings so closely... looking to Jesus the pioneer and perfecter of our faith, who for the sake of the joy that was set before him endured the cross, disregarding its shame, and has taken his seat at the right hand of the throne of God' (Hebrews 12:1b–2).

THE WEIGHT OF SIN

The gravitational pull of divine love draws us up through Jesus to 'the right hand of God', in competition with the gravitational field of the evil in the world and the evil that, in our souls, we call sin. The one gravitational field of the Spirit draws us into God's love and the other field drags us down.

When the astronauts trod on the moon, they found themselves able to leap and jump with ease because gravity on the moon is one-sixth of that on earth. If they had been able to visit Jupiter, they would have crawled on the surface, so strong is the downward force of gravity there. You and I get pulled down all the time. Our bodies, thankfully, get pulled down to stay on earth, but our spirits—they get pulled down too and can feel very heavy.

Human beings are pulled down in the gravitational field of

seven deadly sins: pride, anger, lust, envy, gluttony, avarice and sloth. Someone made up a mnemonic for these sins—'pale gas', indicating their deadly impact through a comparison to chlorine. The deadly sins weigh us down in different ways. For some of us, the heaviness is sloth, or laziness, especially as we get older. For others it's the weight of indulgence through gluttony, or the dead weight of pride that sinks so many of our relationships. Then we have avarice—greed, which can literally weigh us down!

The downward gravity of sin affects us all. When we try to rise above it by our own efforts, we feel as if we are in the gym, trying to lift weights that are beyond our capacity. The more we try to lift ourselves, the heavier life feels. The gravitational field of God's love that lifts our lives can't be felt through our own efforts. It reaches down to offer us a hand up in Jesus and all he has done for us by his life, death and resurrection and the gift of the Holy Spirit.

As we struggle with our relationships, insecurities and spiritual emptiness, we find ourselves caught by the gravitational lure of sin as if in quicksand. The more we struggle in our own strength to release ourselves, the deeper we go down. I remember someone driving his father's Land Rover on to a beach south of Morecambe Bay, where it sank hopelessly into quicksand before he could get a purchase on it. He had some answering to do to his dad! It is a sad truth of life that so many of our attempts to better ourselves prove counterproductive. People caught in quicksand sink *faster* through gravity, the more they struggle to get out of it. They need an upward pull from outside themselves.

Jesus does that for us when we make him our choice, a choice that we seal continuously in praying the Jesus Prayer. Through his resurrection from cruel death, the gravitational pull of God's love has been proved more powerful than the quicksand of sin, death and the devil. The sinful human condition is something we cannot escape from unaided. *We* can't become godlike. *We* can't elevate ourselves beyond the quicksand that drags us down, however hard we try. Jesus can, though: he can make us godlike. He will—if we will let him—provide us with the upward pulls we need, hour by hour, to rise above the heaviness of our human condition into the glorious liberty of the children of God.

I was walking on the South Downs last weekend. It was a windy day and so on my journey I stumbled on a group of hang-gliders assembling to exploit the wind and ride the thermals. One of them explained to me how much patience they required to await just the right moment to launch the gliders, once they had been put together from their enormous backpacks. The potential flyers and their gliders huddled in a field near a car park on the top of the Downs, awaiting their respective moments. It would be a matter of sensing the breeze and then moving their machine a bit down the slope to obtain the needed lift. Once in flight, they would soar on thermal air currents to gain a bird's eye view of one of Britain's greatest landmarks.

It occurred to me that the discipline of being a hang-glider is a parable of the discipline of praying the Jesus Prayer. In this age-old discipline, we teach ourselves to voice inwardly and continuously, 'Lord Jesus Christ, Son of God, have mercy on me, a sinner.' That inner conversation seems one-sided most of the time, but I find it disposes me to receive spiritual uplift that I would miss without the discipline. Like the hang-glider pilot I met as I prayed my way along the Downs, I find myself engaging with many more of God's surprises when I am praying in this way than on the occasions when my spirit is more self-preoccupied. We were made by God for uplift into his possibilities, to attain his viewpoint, but the disposition to be so lifted is as important as the breath of the Holy Spirit who is again and again able to lift us out of ourselves.

In Matthew's Gospel, Jesus tells his followers, 'Keep awake... for you do not know at what hour your Lord is coming' (Matthew 24:42). Praying the Jesus Prayer is a form of attentiveness to the Lord that opens us up to his opportunities and overcomes the weight of our own cares. These cares are put into a right perspective when we are carried into the dynamic of the Holy Spirit, present always and everywhere, who needs us to achieve his purposes. I am more and more convinced that God can't have us for his purposes most times because of our self-regard, and it is this self-regard that a prayer discipline overcomes. It is the root of sin. Only those whose attention is freed from the sinful self can attain God's heights. I think especially of the example of the virgin Mary, without whom God's main plan for the world would have failed, and her capacity to 'magnify the Lord' and to 'treasure in her heart' what she had seen and heard (Luke 1:46; 2:51). The Jesus Prayer is, for lesser mortals than her, a way of countering self-orientation and taking flight through unselfconsciousness into a dynamic of serving the loving purposes of God.

GOD RICH IN MERCY

The phrase 'have mercy on me, a sinner' in the Jesus Prayer echoes both heartfelt prayers to Jesus in the Gospels and a phrase that recurs in Christian worship: *kyrie eleison,* literally 'O Lord, take pity on me'.

*Two blind men followed [Jesus], crying loudly, 'Have mercy on us [*eleison*], Son of David!'* (Matthew 9:27)

*Just then a Canaanite woman from that region came out and started shouting, 'Have mercy on me [*eleison*], Lord, Son of David; my daughter is tormented by a demon.'* (Matthew 15:22)

*When he heard that it was Jesus of Nazareth, [Bartimaeus] began to shout out and say, 'Jesus, Son of God, have mercy on me [*eleison*].'* (Mark 10:47)

The Greek verb *eleeo* used in these texts and in the *kyrie eleison* of Christian worship 'signifies, in general, to feel sympathy with the misery of another, and especially sympathy manifested in act'.[12] There is an association with healing and salvation in both its Gospel and liturgical use, which is carried into the practice of saying the Jesus Prayer. It is an asking for mercy on account of wretchedness, a lift to counter the downward force of circumstances, including sin.

Another Greek verb, *hilaskomai*, is used in the parable of the Pharisee and the tax collector, in Luke 18:9–14:

*[Jesus] also told this parable to some who trusted in themselves that they were righteous and regarded others with contempt: 'Two men went up to the temple to pray, one a Pharisee and the other a tax collector. The Pharisee, standing by himself, was praying thus, "God, I thank you that I am not like other people: thieves, rogues, adulterers, or even like this tax collector. I fast twice a week; I give a tenth of all my income." But the tax collector, standing far off, would not even look up to heaven, but was beating his breast and saying, "God, be merciful [*hilatheti*] to me, a sinner!" I tell you, this man went down to his home justified rather than the other;*

for all who exalt themselves will be humbled, but all who humble themselves will be exalted.'

The verb *hilaskomai* used here 'in profane Greek meant to conciliate, appease, propitiate, cause the gods to be reconciled... in the New Testament the word never means to conciliate God; it signifies... to be propitious, merciful, Luke 18:13... That God is not of himself already alienated from man, see John 3:16 (God so loved the world...). With regard to his sin, an expiation is necessary, consistently with God's holiness and for his righteousness sake, and that expiation his grace and love have provided in the atoning sacrifice of his Son.[13]

The New Testament revelation in Jesus Christ is of 'God, who is rich in mercy' (Ephesians 2:4) and who 'saved us, not because of any works of righteousness that we had done, but according to his mercy' (Titus 3:5a). That mercy is disposed to reach down to those like the tax collector who reckon themselves as nothing, rather than to those like the Pharisee who are over-sure of themselves. It is already evident in the Old Testament, where references to God's mercy, grace and faithfulness more than balance references to God's wrath against sinners. Mercy is seen as an essential practical qualification for authentic worship: 'For I desire mercy, not sacrifice, and acknowledgement of God rather than burnt offerings' (Hosea 6:6, NIV). The practice of mercy is commended by Jesus in the Beatitudes (Matthew 5:7), and his story of the merciless servant who failed to reflect the great mercy shown to him by his master to another servant who is indebted to him paints lack of mercy as a very great vice (Matthew 18:23–35). The Lord's Prayer enshrines the same teaching—that asking God to forgive us our wrongs requires a commitment to forgive those who wrong us (Luke 11:4). 'Be merciful, just as your Father is merciful' (Luke 6:36).

The beautiful impact of living close to God's mercy is captured by the apostle Paul, who reminds the Ephesians of how the deadening gravity of disobedient passion or hopeless self-congratulation for good works is overcome in those who welcome the heavenward lift of Jesus Christ. Knowing our need of mercy is nothing futile, because we were made to receive it and it is freely given to all who rely upon it day by day, hour by hour. This passage is one of the most uplifting in the whole of scripture:

> *You were dead through the trespasses and sins in which you once lived, following the course of this world, following the ruler of the power of the air, the spirit that is now at work among those who are disobedient. All of us once lived among them in the passions of our flesh, following the desires of flesh and senses, and we were by nature children of wrath, like everyone else. But God, who is rich in mercy, out of the great love with which he loved us even when we were dead through our trespasses, made us alive together with Christ—by grace you have been saved—and raised us up with him and seated us with him in the heavenly places in Christ Jesus, so that in the ages to come he might show the immeasurable riches of his grace in kindness toward us in Christ Jesus. For by grace you have been saved through faith, and this is not your own doing; it is the gift of God—not the result of works, so that no one may boast. For we are what he has made us, created in Christ Jesus for good works, which God prepared beforehand to be our way of life.* **(Ephesians 2:1–10)**

To show mercy is to treat others as better than they are. In the Jesus Prayer we are not asking the Lord repeatedly to demonstrate mercy to us so much as affirming and celebrating that quality, allowing it to brush off on us and make us more fully his instruments of forbearance.

A SIMPLE CHOICE

I have sermons to write and sick people to visit, and the monthly parish magazine copy is due today. I have a 'to do' list that haunts me and there is much work to fall into—or fall back to. It's the default position of falling back into the work of the Lord, rather than the Lord of the work, that I need to counter, and the Jesus Prayer is an enormous aid in this. It is good to have drive, but when we are over-driven we lose the enjoyment of life that the lambs in the field demonstrate. Those lambs are my teachers through their God-given joyful freedom.

When you choose God, you recognise that 'you have been saved through faith, and this is not your own doing; it is the gift of God—not the result of works' (Ephesians 2:8–9a). You live with God's mercy—a sense of your own need of it and a readiness to live and so hand on the good news of grace. My strategic gifts help me facilitate and push forward a number of things in my life and the life of St Giles, my church, but they present me with a spiritual danger. I am working for achievement, but woe betide me if that application to achievement so narrows my life down that it shuts me off from family, neighbours or anyone else who wants to spend time with me.

'Lord Jesus Christ, Son of God, have mercy on me, a sinner.' I need mercy to free me at times from sitting in my study, writing pages of a spiritual book, when I can go and receive spiritual benefit outside that realm of application. The strategic approach is best allied with serendipity, the accident of finding something good while not specifically applying yourself to do so. It's not either–or but both–and. The spiritual message of mercy, like those lambs gambolling in the field, has a serendipitous slant. It's not too worked-out or controlled or systematic. 'I will have mercy on whom I have mercy,' says God (Romans 9:15), but we can be disposed or not towards his grace. The workaholic tendency is definitely counter to such a disposition, as it is a tendency to be in control of life, which goes against the Lord of life.

I can think of many occasions when I've been wrested from my achievement-focused routine so that I could receive something. This can happen as simply as it did this morning, when I was on my way to do some study and writing at the British Library in London. All of a sudden I felt impelled to put a book that was irrelevant to my study in my bag along with the iPad. My train journey sped by as I picked up wisdom that felt God-given from that book, finally stopping to read at all but simply enjoying the journey and praying for those around me. As I did so, using the Jesus Prayer, I felt my breathing synchronise with the prayer so that the phrase 'have mercy' came as I breathed out. I became mindful of God's mercy, like his Spirit, enfolding the surrounding tourists and commuters. Somehow my bathing in mercy on the journey turned into a desire for some seemingly fraught people around me to receive the same blessing through God's action in their circumstances. Perhaps it is irrelevant to note that my studies and writing flowed all the better when I finally sat down in the library. What mattered was that my concern to maximise efficient use of time on the day, which might have meant studying on the train, was overcome by the desire to be more conscious of God in the present moment on my journey.

The choice to live for God is a choice to live under mercy and not compulsion. It is an ongoing choice, which the Jesus Prayer can facilitate. Often I see that choice as a putting on of my mental brakes as I hurry to fit more activities in, or to get to more places or people, in the limited time I have. At one level, that is a commendable, whole-hearted desire to serve God and people. At another level, it is frequently culpable, since I am driving myself along without sufficient invitation for God to be working in and through my life. The prayer 'Lord Jesus Christ, Son of God, have mercy on me, a sinner' that I have disciplined myself to use flows continuously, deep within me, to surface with consequence when I wake up to it. Then God's mercy frees me from preoccupation with my own agenda, amusement and achievements, opening me up to take time with him or with whomever he has brought before me to listen to or to serve.

No parable of mercy is more graphic than that told by Jesus in Matthew 18:23–35 of the unmerciful servant. In recent years, I have used this parable as part of my spiritual weaponry against my own lack of mercy towards myself:

The kingdom of heaven may be compared to a king who wished to settle accounts with his slaves. When he began the reckoning, one who owed him ten thousand talents was brought to him; and, as he could not pay, his lord ordered him to be sold, together with his wife and children and all his possessions, and payment to be made. So the slave fell on his knees before him, saying, 'Have patience with me, and I will pay you everything.' And out of pity for him, the lord of that slave released him and forgave him the debt. But that same slave, as he went out, came upon one of his fellow slaves who owed him a hundred denarii; and seizing him by the throat, he said, 'Pay what you owe.' Then his fellow slave fell down and pleaded with him, 'Have patience with me, and I will pay you.' But he refused; then he went and threw him into prison until he would pay the debt. When his fellow slaves saw what had happened, they were greatly distressed, and they went and reported to their lord all that had taken place. Then his lord summoned him and said to him, 'You wicked slave! I forgave you all that debt because you pleaded with me. Should you not have had mercy on your fellow slave, as I had mercy on you?' And in anger his lord handed him over to be tortured until he would pay his entire debt. So my heavenly Father will also do to every one of you, if you do not forgive your brother or sister from your heart.

It is the beauty of the age-old Jesus Prayer that it is a continual reminder both of God's mercy towards me and of my call to imitate it in my dealings towards others and towards myself. The destructive, unkind ruthlessness towards self that we name 'workaholism' is unworthy of a Christian, since, like the unmerciful servant, it acts in forgetfulness of the unmerited mercy that God shows towards us all. Nothing I do can make me more worthy of that mercy, but a lot of what I do—or don't do—can make me unworthy as the channel God wants me to be of the same mercy, whether towards others or towards myself.

In his book *What's So Amazing about Grace?* Philip Yancey quotes Simone Weil's insight into how we fill up those very channels which God yearns to use so that he can bring his grace and mercy into a hurting world:

Weil concluded that two great forces rule the universe: gravity and grace. Gravity causes one body to attract other bodies so that it continually enlarges by absorbing more and more of the universe into itself. Something like this same force operates in human beings. We too want to expand, to acquire, to swell in significance... Emotionally, Weil concluded, we humans operate by laws as fixed as Newton's. 'All the natural *movements of the soul are controlled by laws analogous to those of physical gravity. Grace is the only exception.' Most of us remain trapped in the gravitational field of self-love, and thus we 'fill up the fissures through which grace might pass'.*[14]

Lord Jesus Christ, Son of God, have mercy on me, a sinner.

CHAPTER 3

A simple prayer

History of the Jesus Prayer

In the late summer of 1990 I received a phone call from Coventry. Bishop Simon Barrington-Ward invited me to come and have a chat with him about the possibility of my becoming Vicar of St Luke, Holbrooks. I had just returned from a term of missionary service with the United Society for the Propagation of the Gospel (now called 'Us'), and Bishop Simon's previous involvement in leading the Church Missionary Society (CMS) gave us much to talk about. From my first encounter with this man, I was impressed by a spiritual force beyond him, and, although he came from a definite evangelical background, he gave evidence of a breadth of appreciation that included the Jesus Prayer. For seven years I served under him as parish priest of Holbrooks. Simon's breadth of appreciation, linked to a concern for depth in Christian formation and passion for intercessory prayer, helped to bring Coventry churches of several denominations together monthly on a Sunday evening to pray for the city. In many ways, Bishop Simon Barrington-Ward recovered the legacy of Bishop Cuthbert Bardsley, who prepared for the 1963 consecration of Coventry Cathedral by seeking under God to prepare a 'consecrated people'.[15]

'I am not so interested in whether people are high church or low church as in whether they are deep church' was one of Simon's themes, and his evident Christian devotion added force to those provocative words at a time when the ordination of women was causing shallow behaviour on every side. Whenever I sat down with Simon, I found space and inspiration, not just from the intellectual side of the man but from his heart for intercession: I was very sure that he prayed for me as one of his priests. I took note of his passion to use the Jesus Prayer and encourage others to do the same. This passion led him to work with Brother Ramon SSF on *Praying the Jesus Prayer Together* (BRF, 2001), having already written *The Jesus Prayer* (BRF, 1996), which this book very much complements. I was grateful to Bishop Simon for writing the foreword to my own book, *Meet Jesus* (BRF, 2011), which included a section on the Jesus Prayer: I am expanding upon that section in the book you are reading now.

In *The Jesus Prayer*, Simon Barrington-Ward provides a helpful biblical and historical background to the prayer and chronicles how it is entwined with his own faith story and the stories of many others. He writes at its conclusion:

> *The Jesus Prayer is a participation in the movement of the redemptive love flowing through all things. I believe that the prayer draws us very near to the heart of the universal gospel. I think that is why it has gained such strength in East and West, and why so many people find it a way of being held by that to which they are still reaching out.*[16]

When Simon speaks of the Prayer as 'a participation in the movement of the redemptive love', he expresses perfectly my own experience of it as a devotion that is ecumenical in the best dynamic Spirit-given sense. It is always good when Christian traditions engage and overlap, but dynamic outcomes are quite rare in my experience. (I am probably thinking of attempts to construct services to please all, which fail signally to please any!) The beauty of the Jesus Prayer is the way it has been carried beyond Orthodoxy through its own intrinsic spiritual momentum, appealing as it does to the literal heart of Christian devotion. With the energy it provides, feeding into both worship and intercession, it does indeed 'draw us very near to the heart of the universal gospel'.

THE GOLDEN THREAD

To speak of catholic Christianity means much more than its common or garden interpretation as Roman Catholic. The term 'catholic' which appears in the creeds is rich in Christian significance and comes from the Greek *katholou*, meaning 'according to the whole'. Besides its implications in terms of what is universally held to be Christian faith today, this is a word that looks to wholeness in the sense of what rings true to the faith of the church through the ages, as opposed to mere contemporary fashion. Another aspect of its meaning stresses inclusivity—in other words, the whole gospel held by the whole church to be communicated to the whole world. Yet another emphasises the interconnectedness between prayer, doctrine and ethics, such that the unravelling of the linkage is seen to weaken the impact of Christianity in any age.

We can trace back the faith that Christians hold today, in continuity with the faith taught through the ages, which is symbolised by the succession of bishops from the apostles onward, but there is also another source of cohesion. This is the 'golden thread' of continuity that might be put under the broad heading of 'spiritual direction'. The fact that we exist as Christians today is due to the faithful transmission of Christian worship and teaching, but it is also due to the encouragement to prayerful connecting with Jesus Christ that has been provided by spiritual guides through the centuries. If we are 'catholic' Christians, we are so in the sense of holding both to the worship and faith of the Church taught through the ages and to a robust spiritual tradition, parallel to episcopal succession, that forms Christ's people as a prayerful people. This is particularly symbolised in Eastern Orthodoxy, where each bishop is linked to a religious community and where such communities are seen in close relation to this 'golden thread'. In Orthodoxy, the writings of spiritual fathers and mothers down the ages are granted exceptional authority, as in *The Philokalia,* meaning 'love of the beautiful or good'.[17] This collection of spiritual writings from the fourth to the 15th century, compiled in the 18th century, presents age-old wisdom from 40 teachers, mainly from the monastic tradition within Orthodoxy.

From time to time in my ministry I have been privileged to take time off to resource my spiritual life. In 2007 I spent two months in a remote location in Guyana, reading *The Philokalia* and looking to get a better grasp of this 'golden thread' spanning the Christian centuries. I took with me a prayer rope from my local monastery as a symbol of this thread, for I had already been convinced that repetition of the Jesus Prayer was a gift that God had for me. Encounters with two or three folk, remarkable in my eyes for their joyful goodness and devoted to this Orthodox way of prayer, triggered my openness, along with a fascination for the beauty of the

Orthodox liturgy. Over a period of six weeks, I had space to centre my life, away from any kind of mass media distraction and on to God, through a commitment to draw in wisdom from *The Philokalia* while reciting the Jesus Prayer—one of its major features, tracing back to the fourth-century Desert Fathers.

I was to discover first-hand the truth spoken over 1500 years ago by Hesychius of Jerusalem that 'invocation of the Name of Jesus and freedom from passionate thoughts is indeed a blessed practice, for it brings peace to the soul'.[18] The discipline of repeating to myself, 'Lord Jesus Christ, Son of God, have mercy on me, a sinner' settled my spirit and brought my mind, heart and will into some sort of unification and peace that has never left me.

> *He who wishes to cleanse his heart should call constantly on the Lord Jesus against our mental enemies... [this] agrees with the testimony of the Scriptures: 'Prepare to meet thy God, O Israel' (Amos 4:12)... 'Pray without ceasing' (1 Thessalonians 5:17)... 'He that abides in me, and I in him... brings forth much fruit' (John 15:5).*[19]

The 'golden thread' I write of pulls us through centuries of Christian devotion, down to scriptural injunctions such as these, which invite continuous prayer with an abiding in Christ. In *The Philokalia* the various spiritual teachers come back again and again to the need for prayer to descend from the mind to the heart, and remind us that the recitation of the Jesus Prayer is a proven biblical resource.

This teaching in *The Philokalia* was first drawn to my attention by a friend I made through our being ordained together in Sheffield Cathedral over 35 years ago. A great strength of Anglicanism is its breadth, combining catholic, evangelical, charismatic and radical traditions as if in a four-cylinder engine. Sadly, there is sometimes little engagement between these 'cylinders', but ordinations bring people together across the traditions, and I kept up regularly with Peter, who was a mixture of evangelical and charismatic in that he had fairly recently experienced a filling or baptism in the Holy Spirit and spoke in tongues. To interpret that experience, he had been guided towards the section of *The Philokalia* that speaks of the descent of the mind into the heart, and found it very reassuring to see there an affirmation of his experience as well as guidance. It was his pleasure to guide me through a similar experience over the first years of our ordained ministries and to point me to a vital strand of what I am calling 'the golden thread' of spiritual continuity.

THE WAY OF A PILGRIM

Alongside *The Philokalia* and my prayer rope, I took another resource to Guyana that is famous as a popularisation of the Jesus Prayer. *The Way of a Pilgrim* is a small book by an anonymous author, the text of which was found on Mount Athos and translated from its Russian original to be widely disseminated in the late 19th century.[20] The book, usually published together with its sequel, *The Pilgrim Continues His Way*, tells how the narrator wanders about Russia from one place to another in the years preceding the liberation of the serfs in 1861, and it ranks among the most popular and widely read spiritual classics. The story is either literal history or an invented tale centring on the narrator's desire to follow 1 Thessalonians 5:17 in praying without ceasing. That ambition leads him to a spiritual guide who teaches him to say the

Jesus Prayer continuously and gives him *The Philokalia* to read, so that he can learn how to pray without ceasing:

> *We went into his cell and he began to speak as follows. 'The continuous interior Prayer of Jesus is a constant uninterrupted calling upon the divine name of Jesus with the lips, in the spirit, in the heart; while forming a mental picture of his constant presence, and imploring his grace, during every occupation, at all times, in all places, even during sleep. The appeal is couched in these terms, "Lord Jesus Christ, have mercy on me." One who accustoms himself to this appeal experiences as a result so deep a consolation and so great a need to offer the prayer always, that he can no longer live without it, and it will continue to voice itself within him of its own accord. Now do you understand what prayer without ceasing is?' 'Yes indeed, Father, and in God's name teach me how to gain the habit of it,' I cried, filled with joy. 'Read this book,' he said. 'It is called "The Philokalia", and it contains the full and detailed science of constant interior prayer, set forth by twenty-five holy Fathers... It contains clear explanations of what the Bible holds in secret and which cannot be easily grasped by our short-sighted understanding... Holy Scripture... is a dazzling sun, and this book, "The Philokalia", is the piece of glass which we use to enable us to contemplate the sun in its imperial splendour.'*[21]

This has been my experience. *The Philokalia,* of which *The Way of a Pilgrim* is an intriguing taster, has been a way for me into 'the light of the knowledge of the glory of God in the face of Jesus Christ' (2 Corinthians 4:6b). The Russian pilgrim's persistent desire for continuous prayer became my inspiration, allied to the golden thread of teaching in *The Philokalia,* so I could see with that pilgrim how 'shining through the heart, the light of the name of Jesus illuminates all the universe'.[22]

The popularity of *The Way of a Pilgrim* was boosted by its featuring in J.D. Salinger's bestseller *Franny and Zooey* (Penguin, 1965), in which the college student Franny is fascinated by the book and describes it as a way to see God, with similarities in its spiritual discipline to Eastern meditation techniques (something we will be considering later in this book). What so impressed me about *The Way of a Pilgrim* was its easy readability while dealing with profound, life-changing matters—the sort of unique text that caught Franny's imagination. When you read *The Way of a Pilgrim*, the parallels with Eastern mantra recitation techniques are hardly voiced, of course. It is more focused on the pilgrim's wholehearted quest for union with God and how his quest is set within a discipline of regular attendance at church and submission to the 'golden thread' of spiritual direction, of which *The Philokalia* is part. That determined quest is always balanced by constant reminders of God's quest for us:

> *Of course, God does not need our sinful prayers, but still in his love for us he likes us to pray...* Abide in me, and I in you; *but every intention, every impulse, even every thought which is directed to his glory and our own salvation, is of value in his sight. For all these the bountiful loving kindness of God gives bountiful rewards. The love of God gives grace a thousandfold more than human actions deserve. If you give him the merest mite, he will pay you back with gold. If you but purpose to go to the Father, he will come out to meet you. You say but a word, short and unfeeling—'Receive me, have mercy on me'—and he falls on your neck and kisses you. That is what the love of the heavenly Father is like towards us, unworthy as we are.*[23]

A SIMPLE PRAYER

This last fortnight, my village has been blessed with visits from both the Bishop of Chichester and the Bishop of Guyana. It's been an extraordinary time. Someone said that it's made bishops like London buses: you never see one for ages, then two come at once! Both brought challenge and affirmation, in that one outcome for me was being made a Canon of St George's Cathedral, Guyana. Ecclesiastical honours are rare, since clerics are many and diocesan postings few, so there was elation in me, my family and our church about this surprise of the Spirit. I say 'of the Spirit' since my appointment as the Bishop of Guyana's UK Commissary—one granted authority to act for him in this country—builds on St Giles' support for the Guyana Diocesan Association through my wife Anne and my historic and ongoing links. The email confirming my appointment recalled my years spent training priests there, as well as my ongoing ministry of encouragement to the church in that country.

It lifted my heart to be so honoured, while ringing warning bells about pride and vanity as the interior movement of my spirit, allied to the Jesus Prayer, acted to steady me. I recall how past honours, such as my Chemistry doctorate and ordination, sent me into times of high consolation that probably made me somewhat insufferable to my peers and soon saw me plunged into desolation as my vanities got punctured. It is my experience nowadays that saying the Jesus Prayer keeps me on more of an even keel emotionally, through the default occupation that it gives to my mind and heart. That occupation is, of course, an ongoing act of my will, which is very slowly getting geared to build God's kingdom more than my own. Any idea that the Jesus Prayer is some sort of spiritual 'quick fix' needs challenging. Like all prayer, it is both a gift and an ongoing task. Paul writes, 'Work out your own salvation with fear and trembling...' but then, balancing that teaching, he says immediately, 'for it is God who is at work in you, enabling you both to will and to work for his good pleasure' (Philippians 2:12b–13). The will to persist in saying the Jesus Prayer is mine but not mine, just as our service of God's kingdom (rather than our own kingdom) is ours, but only ours through God's calling.

The Jesus Prayer is a simple prayer, commended by the faith of the church through the ages, and the practice of it is, in my experience, a steering away from things that would complicate my life, emotions, thought and prayer. It is a God-send, even though it does not cease to be hard work, requiring spiritual determination.

Bishop Kallistos writes:

Wherein, we ask, lies the distinctive appeal and effectiveness of the Jesus Prayer? Perhaps in four things above all: first, in its simplicity and flexibility; secondly in its completeness; thirdly, in the power of the Name, and fourthly, in the spiritual discipline of persistent repetition... [completeness in that] there is a circular movement within the Prayer, a sequence of ascent and return. In the first half of the Prayer we rise up to God: 'Lord Jesus Christ, Son of God...'; and then in the second half we return to ourselves in compunction... 'on me a sinner'. 'Those who have tasted the gifts of the Spirit', it is stated in the Macarian Homilies, 'are conscious of two things at the same time: on the one hand, of joy and consolation; on the other, of trembling and fear and mourning.' Such is the inner dialectic of the Jesus Prayer.[24]

In those words Bishop Kallistos explains how what he calls 'the inner dialectic' of this simple prayer brings its own ongoing consolation and desolation, which, I find, detaches me from earthly joys and sorrows. Just as stepping into a jacuzzi to sit bodily in artificially troubled waters settles a troubled mind, so the ongoing recitation of the Jesus Prayer, with its 'up and down' spiritual motion, seems to lead the soul away from damaging elation or depression. The power of this prayer is in its sort of 'godly distraction', which rescues me from an unsavoury focus upon the successes or failures of life. More than that, it helps me rise above my sinful tendencies that (I can be sure) will rest within me to my dying day. This is the repeated counsel of encouragement within *The Philokalia*, as in this advice from the fifth-century teacher and priest, Hesychius of Jerusalem:

> *As it is impossible to cross the expanse of the sea without a large ship, so without calling on Jesus Christ it is impossible to banish from the soul the suggestion of a wicked thought... Invocation of the name of Jesus Christ banishes such thoughts from the heart. As soon as suggestion is formed in the soul by an image of some physical object, such as a man who has wronged us, or a beautiful woman, or silver or gold, or when thoughts of all these things come to us in turn, it immediately becomes clear that these fantasies were brought to our heart by the spirits of ill-will, lust and avarice. If our mind is experienced, trained and accustomed to protect itself from suggestions and to see clearly, as by the light of day, the seductive fantasies and beguilements of the demons, then, by resistance, contradiction and prayer to Jesus Christ, it immediately and easily repels the red-hot arrows of the devil. It does not allow passionate fantasies to entice away*

> *our thoughts and forbids our thoughts to attach themselves to the suggested image or to fraternise and allow it to multiply or to identify with it, for evil deeds follow upon all this as inevitably as night follows day.*[25]

Although such wisdom makes easier reading than employing, it carries profound psychological insight. Our understanding of the world within us is always an achievement as it moves us towards improving that world. The writers of *The Philokalia* were as aware as the psychotherapists of our own day of how our inner life is prey to our passions. Like contemporary psychologists, they also provide strategies to address these 'demons'—of which recitation of the Jesus Prayer is the simplest and allegedly most powerful. A parallel can be drawn between cognitive behavioural therapy, which helps people by shaking them into decisive action for their own well-being, and advice like that above, written in terms of spiritual warfare.[26] What is at issue in both psychotherapy and spiritual direction is how we can best change our thinking and our behaviour for good—or for God, so we grow into 'the measure of the full stature of Christ' (Ephesians 4:13).

Hesychius and the so-called 'Hesychasts', who are key authors within *The Philokalia,* were masters of inner stillness. The Greek *hesychasmos* comes from *hesychia,* which is translated variously as stillness, rest, quiet or silence. This contemplative tradition draws authority from the teaching of Jesus in Matthew 6:6: 'Whenever you pray, go into your room and shut the door and pray to your Father who is in secret; and your Father who sees in secret will reward you.' The traditions of hesychasm are gaining ground in the church today, over and against Christian activism, or maybe sheer workaholism, through the resurgence of contemplative prayer. This has meant a drawing on the wisdom of the church through the ages about how we rise above our senses to contemplate God in quietness.

The hermit traditions were not uncontroversial, since prayer touches on everything and God most of all. The way we talk about our experience of God owes a lot to thinking from those days, built on arguments about such experience. A distinction emerged between God's energies, which we experience by his Spirit, and his essence, which lies beyond human knowledge. St Gregory of Palamas (1296–1359) made this distinction, and it rings true to contemporary psychology in that although we may know and experience people closely, especially our spouses, there always remains something about them that is unknowable or known to them alone.

As I have already suggested, it is to the Eastern Christian tradition of Orthodoxy that we owe the promotion of the Jesus Prayer across the universal church today. This tradition has never seen reformation, which may be linked to its ongoing faithfulness to the plain sense of scripture. Recitation of the Jesus Prayer is evangelical—a simple statement of gospel truth—but also catholic, coming from proven exercise of the church's devotion through the centuries. It remains a simple prayer, however complicated in origin—a gift on offer and a task invited that is timely as Christianity shapes up and refocuses at the beginning of its third millennium.

CHAPTER 4

A simpler mentality

Tackling mental distractions

I spent part of Sunday afternoon at Speakers' Corner in Hyde Park. One of the advantages of living close to London is that, just as my parishioners commute to work, I as parish priest can commute there from my village for recreation. It fascinates me to join in debates that stretch my brain cells. Atheists, Christians, Muslims and Marxists all engage in Hyde Park as part of the freedom of expression that is distinctive of our democratic culture. Issues in debate this week included the army's removal of the Egyptian president and the perceived incapacity of Islamic leaders to form broad coalitions of interest. As I left the strident debate, one of the more engaging characters I'd met took me to one side and confided that he was a Coptic Christian from Egypt and had appreciated my contribution. Suddenly the intellectual discussion took a back seat to a personal encounter with a believer under persecution. I walked on through Hyde Park to attend a church service with him on my heart.

As I walked, the Jesus Prayer was, as ever, my companion, settling my mind, centring me on God and his love for the Sunday crowds picnicking around me, preparing me for the sung evening prayer that I was due to attend at a church in Knightsbridge.

'By love he is holden, not by thought,' wrote the medieval author of *The Cloud of Unknowing* in a text that recommends repetition of a single holy word to settle the mind, so that the heart can reach out to God 'with the eager dart of longing love'.[27] This wisdom builds from the age-old Christian tradition of meditation, of which the Jesus Prayer is typical, and gives a brutal reminder about the limits of thought: it can be slippery, vapid and distracting from what is ultimately important. Love is more concrete, though it often follows careful thinking, and, by contrast, grasps God and the concerns of God so as to make a difference, not least through prayer.

My experience in Hyde Park demonstrates the way my mind burns with ideas to be debated internally and externally, a debating that needs again and again to give way to something more profound. Just as meeting that Egyptian Christian had an impact on me over and above the intellectual debate about his country's politics, so my personal encounter with God is brought about by the Jesus Prayer as it takes me deeper than purely mental reflection. Such reflection can be highly distracting: an overactive mind has been compared variously to a cloud of mosquitoes buzzing round or to a colony of monkeys leaping from tree to tree. The discipline of reciting the Jesus Prayer provides what I am calling a simpler mentality—in other words, one that sees the periodic clearing of the mind, with useless thoughts put to one side and a centring on what actually matters here and now.

On my Sunday afternoon walk, I moved from thinking and debating to interceding and worshipping through the unfolding of events. Those events had included an important personal encounter, which got me praying for someone at the sharp end of things. The encounter was a trigger for intercession in which my default recitation of the Jesus Prayer came to the surface, replacing and so silencing my thoughts, so that my heart could rest more on God and neighbour. When I arrived before the altar of the Knightsbridge church, I had people on my heart to bring before God for blessing.

COOLING THE MIND

'Long labour in prayer and considerable time are needed for a man with a mind which never cools to acquire a new heaven of the heart where Christ dwells, as the Apostle says: "Know ye not your own selves, how that Jesus Christ is in you...?" (2 Corinthians 13:5)' So wrote St John of Karpathus in the seventh century,[28] whose advice I particularly appreciate, as I am such 'a man with a mind which never cools', seeking 'to acquire that heaven of the heart' which has Christ's indwelling. In the Jesus Prayer I have found a check to useless cerebral activity that helps the circumstances of the present moment to break into my psyche, warm my heart and help it move, however untidily, towards the heart of God.

The repeating of the prayer is not the 'vain repetition' condemned by Jesus in Matthew 6:7 (KJV). Rather, it is a warding off of vain mental preoccupation, once the Jesus Prayer is given permission by the will to surface from its default interior cogitation. 'Lord Jesus Christ, Son of God, have mercy on me, a sinner': the sentence takes hold of us and does away with negativity. As I was writing just now, the phone rang and I listened for 20 minutes to a man angered by dealings that have been salt in the wound of a raw and tragic bereavement. That conversation has touched my spirit and distracted my mind, causing me to wonder what, if anything, I can do to help his healing. Even though I am back at the computer, my mind and heart are with him, yet I sense the Jesus Prayer flowing in me, cleansing me inside. As Paul wrote, 'If Christ is in you, though the body is dead because of sin, the Spirit is life because of righteousness. If the Spirit of him who raised Jesus from the dead dwells in you, he who raised Christ from the dead will give life to your mortal bodies also through his Spirit that dwells in you' (Romans 8:10–11).

The Jesus Prayer, containing as it does the Saviour's name, is something redeeming, as there is a close association between name and person in biblical understanding. For the Jews of the Old Testament, knowing someone's name brought them close to all that that person was about, and the name of Jesus, for Christians, stands for entry into the heart of God himself. Our minds can conjure up thoughts and images that deceive us and take us away from where we are meant to be heading, which is towards God. Like the phone call I received, all kinds of things come at us and upset our spiritual equilibrium, so we need help to maintain our balance. Taking a deep breath and finding something to take your mind off the distractions—in my case, writing this book—are helpful strategies, and the Jesus Prayer is a profound part of those strategies in my experience. 'Let the same mind be in you that was in Christ Jesus,' says Paul (Philippians 2:5). Invoking the name of Jesus places me in God's presence and opens my heart to his energy as I voice inside myself an ongoing desire to surrender myself to God's mercy.

This is a very powerful dynamic, such that recalling the holy name of Jesus seems very often to bring God's power into play within my situation.

The release of the mind into the heart is key to holy living, as it helps our thoughts and indeed our wills to submit to the work that God has for us and, through us, for a needy world. Repeating the Jesus Prayer is a means to this end, although it is a costly exercise because it involves continual use of the mind, which generates some natural resistance and sometimes a literal pain in the head. The internal flow of our thoughts is impossible to control fully but there are ways of disengaging ourselves and rising above that flow—and to this end the Jesus Prayer is a great servant.

Elder Thaddeus of Vitovnica became one of the most famous spiritual guides within 20th-century Serbian Orthodoxy. *Our Thoughts Determine Our Lives* is the title of a recently published collection of his teachings and it is a telling title indeed. Thaddeus ministered in war-torn Serbia through two World Wars, totalitarian Communism and finally the NATO bombings of 1999, which came just before his death in 2002. 'We cannot achieve salvation in any way other than by transforming our mind, making it different from what it was,' he wrote. 'Our minds become deified by a special act of God's grace. They become passionless and holy. A deified mind is one which lives in remembrance of God at all times. Knowing that God is in us and we in him, the deified mind is perfectly at home with God. He is everywhere, and we are like fish in water when we are in God. The minute our thoughts abandon him, we perish spiritually.'[29] Elder Thaddeus saw the Jesus Prayer as a gift and vital tool in attaining life and joy in God. He wrote:

They taught me how to pray the Jesus Prayer [at Milijko Monastery]. I prayed all the time, and it often happened that although I might have been engaged in conversation with another person, I still heard the words of the Jesus Prayer, which came from my heart on their own. I felt indescribable joy, and there was nothing that could make me angry. Thoughts about the things of this world had no place in my heart as I was in a state of grace. Let us remember the state that the Most Holy Mother of God was in. She lived in the grace of the Holy Spirit all her life.[30]

To Thaddeus, and to many practitioners of the Jesus Prayer, it is a vehicle of gaining the grace that Mary, mother of Jesus, experienced. Jesus, who lived fully in her, lives fully in us by the Spirit so as to fill our thoughts. This vehicle, Thaddeus teaches, is inseparable from the disciplines of attending the Eucharist, confessing our sins, and so on. We should remember that the gift and task of the Jesus Prayer cannot be separated from the corporate life of Christians.

MINDFULNESS

I know a businessman who was sent on a course of Buddhist meditation to improve his performance in the workplace. The commercial world tends to focus on Buddhism as a source of expertise in healthy spiritual practice as far as its teaching on mindfulness is concerned. A fellow priest worked out that there were more people enrolled annually on Buddhist meditation courses in Brighton than attended parish churches. In my view, it is quite extraordinary how people are giving authority for spiritual expertise to Eastern religions over against Christianity (which is, arguably, itself an Eastern religion), and this was one of my prompts for writing this book. In my experience, the Jesus Prayer is among many gifts that we can offer, from the treasury of Christian devotion, to engage with those seeking to build their interior life in the materialistic culture we inhabit. Like other forms of Eastern devotion, it involves a repeated prayer phrase, called a 'mantra' in Eastern traditions, which has the effect of focusing and simplifying the mind's operation.

The Buddha's promotion of so-called 'mindfulness' (*sati-patthana* in the original Sanskrit) stressed the value of awareness of the present moment, and our thoughts and feelings in that moment, as a liberating discernment. This practice of mindfulness or awareness is now being employed by psychologists to treat addiction, depression, anxiety and a number of related conditions. It has much in common with the teaching of Jesus Christ in the Sermon on the Mount, where he exhorts us to contemplate nature as a means of detaching ourselves from an unhealthy preoccupation with self-preservation.

> *'Therefore I tell you, do not worry about your life, what you will eat or what you will drink, or about your body, what you will wear. Is not life more than food, and the body more than clothing? Look at the birds of the air; they neither sow nor reap nor gather into barns, and yet your heavenly Father feeds them. Are you not of more value than they? And can any of you by worrying add a single hour to your span of life? And why do you worry about clothing? Consider the lilies of the field… strive first for the kingdom of God and his righteousness, and all these things will be given to you as well. So do not worry about tomorrow, for tomorrow will bring worries of its own. Today's trouble is enough for today.'* **(Matthew 6:25–28, 33–34)**

This remedy for anxiety, similar to the mental distraction taught in Buddhist-type mindfulness exercises, is offered here by Christ and made available through Christian meditation, especially through the 'God-given mantra' of the Jesus Prayer. Repeating the phrase inwardly is a means of settling mind and spirit in the present moment. The wisdom of both Buddhism and Christianity is that thoughts of both past and future, however much they have an impact on us, are just that—thoughts gathered into mental constructs, of whatever shape. The choice to live in the present moment is affirmed in meditation, and Christianity recognises that God is in that moment alone, by his Spirit. He may have been with us in the past and promises to be with us in the future, but the only moment that we can be sure God actually inhabits is the present moment. Although he acts in time, he is not contained there but is present at the moment-by-moment intersection of time and eternity, meaning that, in Paul's phrase, 'now is the day of salvation' (2 Corinthians 6:2b). Through the discipline of applying the mind to reciting a mantra, we keep our attention on the present moment and free ourselves from both regret about the past and anxiety about the future. While, in atheistic Buddhism, this detachment or mindfulness is the sole source of energy, in Christianity there is an energising attachment alongside this detachment—an attachment or mindfulness towards God.

Anthony de Mello describes a form of prayer developed among Hindus that parallels the ceaseless repetition of the Jesus Prayer, called 'Remembrance of the Name'. He writes:

> *Mahatma Gandhi, who was a zealous advocate of this form of prayer, claimed that it brought with it the most extraordinary benefits for spirit and mind and body. He claimed to have*

overcome all his fears, even as a child, simply through the ceaseless repetition of God's name. He said that there was more power in its recitation than in the atom bomb... according to him, reciting God's name with faith would cure a man of any disease whatsoever. Only he must recite the Name with all his heart and soul and mind during the time of prayer. Outside the time of prayer even a mechanical recitation of the Name will do. Through this seemingly mechanical recitation the Name gets into one's bloodstream, as it were, into the very depths of one's unconscious and of one's being—and very subtly but surely, one's heart and life are transformed.[31]

Gandhi's witness, relayed by Father de Mello, is impressive and opens up a number of questions about how prayer to God, however he is seen, unites people to some degree right across faith traditions. Gandhi's last emphasis touches on the important relationship between formal and informal use of such means of prayer. The time we spend daily putting heart and soul into recitation, with no other employment, feeds into the more mechanical use over the rest of the day, which seems to build from formal prayer time (something we shall consider later as we look in a more detailed way at the practice of praying the Jesus Prayer). It is significant, though, that when we pray the Jesus Prayer we put ourselves alongside not just the devotion of Christians through the ages but also the devotion of other men and women who have found spiritual depth from holy repetition. As in Gandhi's case, this repetition can result in an overcoming of fear and a healing that spreads forth from the practitioner.

A SIMPLER MENTALITY

In his book on the Jesus Prayer, Bishop Simon Barrington-Ward writes:

> *The phrases of the Jesus Prayer give the top of our mind something to be occupied with, so that the rest of the mind can be open to the deeper feeling that lies underneath. This is what those who have used the prayer have called putting the mind in the heart. The words occupy our surface being at the same time as they communicate with the depths in us.*[32]

This is an excellent description of the simpler mentality we are introduced to, whereby the mind is given holy distraction so as to allow prayer from the depth of our being.

In my own experience, the Jesus Prayer has built partly from recitation of the rosary, which I have used as a tool for intercessory prayer over most of my life. The beauty of the rosary is that it is an easily memorised construction of set prayers that can be recited with mind and lips while we allow the heart to focus on aspects of Jesus Christ and relate them to the human needs around. All through my life, my mind has been somewhat overactive, so settling my mind is a challenge when I pray. This is why the rosary has always been valuable to me: I find it to be a way of employing my mind in a work of prayer and spiritual transformation. If I am waiting in a long shopping queue, sensing the impatience in me and around me, I turn the situation to good by deciding to offer the Sorrowful Mysteries of the Rosary. Five times I recite one 'Our Father', ten 'Hail Mary's and one 'Glory to the Father' with my heart respectively on Christ's agony in the garden, scourging, crowning with thorns, carrying of the cross and crucifixion. As I use my mind, the quiet movement of my lips and the finger-counting to recite the rosary for 15 to 20 minutes, my heart is on the successive aspects of Christ's passion. It is also on five people selected from the shopping queue, for whom I offer prayer. In this way of praying the rosary, I choose to let go of deliberately thinking the prescribed words and, in effect, engage in mechanical recitation while praying from the heart, linking to Christ and human need.

Where the Jesus Prayer differs from this form of the rosary is in the significance you are bound to give to reciting the words 'Lord Jesus Christ, Son of God, have mercy on me, a sinner'. These words are meant to occupy you fully as you pray, even if they could be seen as a form of distraction to what Bishop Simon called 'the top of our mind'. Unlike my personal use of the rosary, it is not a matter of setting your mind to pray for 20 minutes while your heart occupies itself with less mechanical prayer. The Jesus Prayer is a gift and task that is for 24/7 use, not 20 minutes—one that is simple yet far-reaching, pulling mind, heart, body and neighbourhood, even cosmos, *together* into prayer. I can, of course, decide to offer the Jesus Prayer for those in a shopping queue, but it is more a matter of offering myself generally on their behalf in union with the perpetual intercession of Jesus, which is within me for them and for the whole world.

The simplification of prayer is something we can barely achieve ourselves. It is given to us at various junctions. As a spiritual director, I am privileged to accompany a number of people on their journey of discipleship, and this gives me insight into the rich variety of aids to Christian devotion beyond the basics of reading the Bible and attending the Eucharist. The Jesus Prayer is an aid to prayer that I have commended over the years, but, although I used to say it occasionally, it had not fully grasped me until I received it as a gift from God seven years ago.

Elder Thaddeus recalls a young man from Bosnia who (like me at first) prayed the Jesus Prayer dutifully but without a deep sense of ownership. This youth told another young friend about the prayer and, in consequence, the friend came to be powerfully transformed. He approached the Elder to share about it and seek his advice:

'Father, it is as though I have been enlightened by a special kind of joy and a peace I cannot describe. In my heart I constantly hear the words, "Lord Jesus Christ, Son of God, have mercy on me, a sinner." I know what I was like before, the kinds of thoughts that I had, but now there is nothing like that in my mind any more. I used to have lustful thoughts for the opposite sex; I used to get angry for the slightest reason, but now… I just cannot get angry… an ineffable joy has taken over my whole being.'

Elder Thaddeus told him he had been given the gift of grace, and that he would have it for as long as he could keep his thoughts away from the cares of this world.

If he were to do that… he would stop hearing the words of the Jesus Prayer in his heart, and then the joy and peace would gradually disappear. He would again become laden with the cumbersome thoughts generated by the prince of this world. I told him that if he wished to keep the gift of Grace he had been given, he was to pray to God ceaselessly in order to block the thoughts that come from the realm of the demons and thus preserve the joy and peace that he was feeling.[33]

The advice that Elder Thaddeus provides to the second young man is a salutary reminder. We can never simplify our lives so as to escape spiritual warfare. This is what Paul also said to the new Christians in Corinth: 'For the weapons of our warfare are not merely human, but they have divine power to destroy strongholds. We destroy arguments and every proud obstacle raised up against the knowledge of God, and we take every thought captive to obey Christ' (2 Corinthians 10:4–5). To take every thought captive, we need a holy will, the central agent of our being, a will that is fortified by cooperation with the divine will and its astonishing power. Since the Jesus Prayer is itself a statement of divine truth, it has power beyond itself, not least through the fact that it contains the name of the Saviour.

Our thoughts determine our lives and they are influenced by where and how we direct them. As I write this book, I feel I have been changed from my resemblance to the first young man in Elder Thaddeus's story, to become more like his graced friend. I began this chapter by describing my interest in public debate, something dear to me, and how the outcome of my thinking and discussing touched my spirit and led me to pray for persecuted Christians. Whether we like it or not, there is a battle for minds going on all around us. That conflict has the power to engage or deflate our spirits, depending on our vigilance on the battlefield as well as the power of our spiritual weaponry. It has been my experience over the last seven years that taking my thoughts 'captive for Christ' is greatly assisted by the practice of praying the Jesus Prayer. Like the second young man described by Elder Thaddeus, I find that some thoughts that formerly preoccupied me are hardly able to gain purchase through the shield I am given in unceasing prayer. In God's presence, moreover, or even in God's mention, there is a joy that, by contrast, *does* gain purchase, as well as spreading out to others.

I suppose I would not be saying the Jesus Prayer if I had not met practitioners, like Bishop Simon, who had something about them that I wanted deep down and who made me open to welcoming the gift and the task when the invitation came. Ironically, that invitation came on a sabbatical (or study leave) which was devoted officially to intellectual study of the Orthodox prayer tradition. From all the words I studied during that leave in Guyana, it was just twelve words that stuck—and, in sticking within me, they became a shield against harmful preoccupation as well as a Spirit-given source of joy: 'Lord Jesus Christ, Son of God, have mercy on me, a sinner.'

CHAPTER 5

A simpler worship

Linking worship and life

Today started with my prayer hour, including a good stretch of quietly repeating the Jesus Prayer. With the momentum of that prayer still moving within me, I went down to church to celebrate the school leavers' Eucharist. This morning I was particularly aware of the Eucharist as a way of entrusting sinners to God's merciful love and of how our lives grow, change and deepen. In blessing the twelve leavers, I've been reminded of how my own life has moved on, as it's been lived much longer than theirs, and of how prayer is gaining a stronger hold on my life. From my teenage years, the Eucharist has been a spiritual focus for me, though I have too often entered into or celebrated it inadequately. In recitation of the Jesus Prayer, I have found a simpler worship that better brings me to the Eucharist and better brings the Eucharist to bear on the routine of my life. That God's love is present to me and to all things is a notion in my mind that's becoming real to my heart and will, and this formation comes from corporate worship and personal prayer. The Jesus Prayer carries me with reverence into the eucharistic offering and carries me out into the world in the extension of my Holy

Communion. Today, also, I feel held after the Eucharist by the emotion expressed among the leavers who have been touched by the liturgy and by the end-of-year awards at our close-knit church primary school.

The centrality of the Eucharist to life is captured in *The Philokalia*, which, as we have seen, is also a major resource on the Jesus Prayer:

> *The greatest help and assistance in purification of the soul, illumination of the mind, sanctification of the body and a Divine transformation of the two, as well as in repulsing passions and demons and, above all, in transubstantial union with God, in joining and merging with Him, is frequent communion in the holy, pure, immortal and life-giving mysteries—the precious body and blood of our Lord Jesus Christ, Our God and Saviour—approached with a heart and disposition as pure as is possible for man.*[34]

My own experience is that, when well prepared for, daily Holy Communion has a positive transformative impact on me. I would strongly endorse the words quoted in *The Philokalia* from Sinai mystic St John of the Ladder: 'If a body coming into contact with another body undergoes a change under its influence, how can a man not change if he touches the body of God with pure hands?'[35]

Back to my day: prayer time, Eucharist, then to my desk, where two fierce emails present themselves. Am I going to lose the peace I have gained through worship and prayer? Here is the battle of faith, and I wage it with an eye to the Lord who has just come to me in the sacrament. 'Lord Jesus Christ, Son of God, have mercy on me, a sinner.' The prayer seems reinforced by the company of Jesus crucified, so that I can rise above suspicious thoughts about my correspondents and find direction. A couple of phone calls and the chance visit to the Rectory of a wise church member supply me with insight to answer the emails in such a way as to open up a bigger picture and appeal for more Christian generosity.

As peace returns with an empty inbox, I rejoice in the way the grace of God has found a bit more bearing in my life. Looking back over the years, vexed parishioners used to do me much more damage than they do today. There is a force within me that resists letting vexation gain purchase in myself, and I recognise that force behind both Holy Communion and recitation of the Jesus Prayer. I am a sinner in need of grace, and I grow grateful even for being reminded of this through things like the tussle of answering difficult emails.

I go back to church for more worship, as the end of term is made the pretext for a big family gathering to bury the ashes of great-grandma Beatrice. Once again, the Jesus Prayer leads me in and out of friendly engagement with a family I know well and the short burial service with its blessing gesture, sprinkling holy water on the remains. There are few more telling signs of mortality than a box of human ashes, and to see her family members sprinkling Bea's remains speaks of the merciful love that enfolds us now and always in our frailty, an insight encapsulated in the Jesus Prayer.

From the burial register, I move on to my last appointment of the day, with a young man decided upon confirmation, with an admirably patient faith pilgrimage. Years of fairly regular Sunday attendance have led to something moving within him, and he has agreed to speak of that regeneration when the bishop visits to confirm him. One of the greatest privileges of being a priest is being party to such revelations concerning the interior life. Hearing of the Holy Spirit's movement in others has often helped me sense the Spirit's movement afresh within myself. 'Lord Jesus Christ, Son of God, have mercy on me, a sinner': that prayer rises afresh within me as I hear the confirmation candidate express his need of mercy and how Jesus has lit up his vision of God.

My day draws to a close with said Evensong, dutiful yet profound, for through this day I have been carried along by the Jesus to whom I have been praying. Through sorrow and joy, worship and more mundane activities, I sense cohesion and continuity. My life and worship are simplified because I am in the company of one in whom 'all things hold together' (Colossians 1:17b). That accompaniment is a gift of God, given especially in the Eucharist and woven into my life and circumstances by the Jesus Prayer.

WORSHIP AND LIFE

Facing death is the ultimate means of concentrating the mind, and last week I was privileged to talk on the phone with a priest colleague who is doing just that as his cancer moves fast forward. In that conversation I found myself very aware of Keith's humility, which was allied to a strong conviction about worship. Sensing that it might be our last conversation, the exchange we had was of mutual praise and encouragement and ended with his saying, 'In the end, all that matters is worship.' Although no longer able to celebrate the Eucharist, he was buoyed up by a vision of what is to come when God is all in all to his saints beyond the confines of this world. I left that conversation awed and much encouraged.

There was worship in heaven before you or I were thought

of, and there will be worship in heaven when our bodies lie in their graves. The good news of Jesus is primarily out of this world, news of 'the resurrection of the body and the life of the world to come' (Nicene Creed). This world is a preparation for heavenly worship, of which our gathering with the risen Lord and his people on Sunday, the day of resurrection, is the anticipation and foretaste. It is not just the summit of the week but a pointer to our life's summit, as the writer to the Hebrews makes very clear in words that are seen as a sermon to early-second-century Christian worshippers:

> *You have come to Mount Zion and to the city of the living God, the heavenly Jerusalem, and to innumerable angels in festal gathering, and to the assembly of the firstborn who are enrolled in heaven, and to God the judge of all, and to the spirits of the righteous made perfect, and to Jesus, the mediator of a new covenant, and to a sprinkled blood that speaks a better word than the blood of Abel.* **(Hebrews 12:22–24)**

If only Sunday worship had that sort of sense (and it can), so that each weekend we renewed the heavenly perspective of which Hebrews writes—of being 'surrounded by so great a cloud of witnesses', laying aside 'every weight and the sin that clings so closely', and running 'with perseverance the race that is set before us, looking to Jesus the pioneer and perfecter of our faith, who for the sake of the joy that was set before him endured the cross, disregarding its shame, and has taken his seat at the right hand of the throne of God' (12:1–2).

In Christianity, worship is inseparable from the vision of what is to come in heaven and of what anticipates it, like a kind of preview, in the church's liturgy. It is also about the life-offering of individuals, 'a sacrifice of praise to God, that is, the fruit of lips that confess his name' (Hebrews 13:15). The beauty of the Jesus Prayer is in its promotion of that life-offering with the confession of the name of God's Son, Jesus Christ, which is essential to worship and the Christian life. It is not the only way we can prepare for corporate worship, but it has the advantage of holding us hour by hour in an attitude that so readily fits the Sunday or weekday hours of corporate Christian worship.

Worship in church doesn't just happen. It flows from the gathering up to God of heartfelt individual devotion, even if it is further excited in that gathering by scripture, sacrament, preaching, testimony and silence through which there is corporate engagement with God. In preparation, worship leaders—priests and musicians—can do their best, but, in my experience, if those attending are not well disposed spiritually, it feels more like a sort of treacle-stirring. A recent teaching document by Roman Catholic bishops gives a reminder of how important the spiritual preparation of Sunday worshippers is as a component in conveying a sense of God's presence within the weekly gathering:

> *The active participation of the faithful is first of all internal in that their thoughts reflect what they hear, do, and say during the liturgy. It is also external in that through their outward bearing and gesture they express their inner participation in the liturgy. The ritual interplay of the internal and external elements of the liturgy conveys the transcendence and the immanence of the living God whom the assembly worships.*[36]

The Jesus Prayer is in itself a life-offering as it affirms God's merciful love shown in Jesus. In naming Jesus, we join ourselves by implication with all who are likewise united with him, in this world and the next. This supremely fits us for corporate worship, in which our individual offering is made one with Christ's. Already, as we pray the Jesus Prayer, repeating God's name brings us into his presence and makes us one with all who look to Christ in worship:

> *In pronouncing the name of Jesus we inwardly meet all them that are united with Our Lord, all them of whom he said: 'where two or three are gathered together in my name, there am I in the midst of them'... Where Jesus is, there is the church. If the invocation of the holy name is a means of union with Our Lord, it is also a means of union with that church which is in him and which no human sin can touch.*[37]

My colleague Keith is now housebound and unable to attend worship, and that brings me sadness at a human level. As we spoke, I was reminded of his strong faith in Jesus Christ, through whom he was making sense, as best he could, of his approaching death. In that conversation his last word to me was of the priority of worship and God's all-embracing mercy. As I reflect on our conversation, I recognise how the Jesus Prayer, with its worship and entreating of God's mercy, is, of all my Christian disciplines, the one most likely to support me on the day when I will be in Keith's situation.

A SIMPLER WORSHIP

They say life is getting complicated. It has probably always been so, but the abundance of choice in Western culture is definitely a complication. From the Christian vantage point, we are more aware than ever of the varieties of catholic and evangelical, charismatic and radical spiritual practices which provide the means of growing as Christian disciples but can cause a certain confusion.

My own Christian discipleship started with confirmation training at boarding school, geared to boys coming of age and including a section on 'The Facts of Life'! Its outcome was a Sunday obligation of sorts, so I began to value gathering for Holy Communion with the Lord's people as a right marker of the Lord's day. When I was at university in Oxford, I met Fr John Hooper, who brought Christianity alive for me and, by his example, preaching and counsel, opened up Anglo-Catholicism for me—a portal into God's majesty, beauty and holiness. I started making my sacramental confession. Some years later, through a faith crisis, I engaged with the charismatic renewal movement and welcomed gifts of the Spirit such as speaking in tongues. In recent years it has been the Eastern Orthodox tradition that has drawn me, as a robust Christian tradition suited to discipleship in an unbelieving culture. I am ending up as a strange mixture of catholic, evangelical, pentecostal and orthodox.

Over the 50 years since my confirmation, worship at the Eucharist and daily prayer have been my highest priority, supplemented by reading the Bible, self-examination and regular confession, spiritual direction, financial giving, intercession and the disciplines of care for others and sharing my faith. In all this, I have found in recent years that the Jesus Prayer is a God-given connector and simplifier.

What a blessing to find a discipline that integrates rather than complicates things! One that helps worship to feed prayer, and prayer to feed into worship; one that helps what I believe, how I worship and the way I behave to find more coherence. Such blessings have come my way through accepting the invitation to repeat constantly, 'Lord Jesus Christ, Son of God, have mercy on me, a sinner.'

In the Orthodox liturgy, the Greek chant *kyrie eleison* is a joyful refrain that pervades the eucharistic celebration, reaching up in gratitude to God's merciful love shown to us in Jesus Christ. In the Anglican and Roman Catholic Eucharists, direct invocation of that mercy shown in Jesus Christ occurs in the 'Lord, have mercy', 'Glory to God' and 'Lamb of God' chants, as well as in the confession, prayer of humble access and intercessions. Through the personal discipline of the Jesus Prayer, those public affirmations of worship continue in and from the heart between Eucharists. With that devotion comes great grace as, in public worship and personal prayer, 'God abides in those who confess that Jesus is the Son of God, and they abide in God' (1 John 4:15).

The Jesus Prayer has power to simplify worship because it is no less than a précis of the Eucharist, as the greatest prayer of Jesus Christ for us to the Father in the merciful love of the Holy Spirit. That prayer and sacrifice form prayerful sacrificial disciples into a new humanity, shaped by his gift to us and the gift we make to one another through, with and in him.

In his book *The Mind of Christ in Worship*, T.F. Torrance expands on how one and the same Spirit is, in Christ, acting as priest in the worship of heaven and in the midst of those gathering in his name as earthly worshippers.

> *It is because he who is Priest, Altar and Offering indivisibly in himself dwells in his church through the Spirit who unites us to him, that the church of believers is constituted the temple or sanctified sphere in which Christ fulfils his ministry as Apostle and High Priest of our confession.*

Torrance explains, building from the letter to the Hebrews, how Jesus has such kinship with us, sharing our human experiences and weaknesses, that he can take us up and sanctify our lives as we join them to his own perfect self-offering to God the Father.

> *As High Priest of our souls Jesus Christ presides through the Spirit in all our liturgical acts in his name, in such a way that while he is offered by us in prayer to the Father, in reality it is he who offers us to the Father in the identity of himself as Offerer and Offering.*[38]

This eloquent summary of the prayer of the Eucharist captures for me something of the dynamic of the Jesus Prayer as, in Simon Barrington-Ward's words, a participation in the movement of the redemptive love flowing through all things.

I have made the most of the complicated diversity of 21st-century Christianity, and I have had to do so in my roles as diocesan mission officer and parish priest in a broad church. The danger I have always recognised in a broad church is that self-selected disciplines can pander to self. I cannot guarantee that opting for repetition of the Jesus Prayer will preserve you from self-indulgence, yet the focus it provides does seem to both simplify and ward off a self-focus. 'Those who confess that Jesus is the Son of God… abide in God' (1 John 4:15), which is true of both the worship of the Eucharist and this prayer.

Affirming Jesus as the Lord of life is a simple affirmation, common to both Eucharist and Jesus Prayer, that implies both self-offering and a readiness to be offered in worship and service by God. Moreover, invoking Jesus' name in prayer is like a sacrament, an outward rite providing inward grace. Bishop Kallistos Ware writes, 'God's name is intimately linked with his person, and so the invocation of the divine name possesses a sacramental character, serving as an efficacious sign of his invisible presence and action.'[39]

The name of Jesus is the Saviour's name. To call upon it at Eucharist or in personal prayer is never without effect, since 'those who confess that Jesus is the Son of God… abide in God'. Through the Jesus Prayer, the gift of Christ, given through the signs of bread and wine at the Eucharist, is continued as 'an interior Eucharist' so that corporate worship flows into personal prayer and back again.

At this morning's Eucharist, we read the parable of the shepherd who went in search of the lost sheep. Since then, the communion that Jesus gave me in bread and wine has been carried through my day, giving me a heart for those around me who are 'like sheep without a shepherd'. Through the Jesus Prayer I am voicing to God, in their midst, faith in his merciful love. It has not seemed necessary so far today to speak to anyone of that love, but, by the practice of this prayer, I am being kept attentive to such opportunities. In this way, day by day, worship and life flow a little more into one another with less disconnection and greater coherence. This is simpler worship and it is God's gift to me through the Jesus Prayer.

CHAPTER 6

A simpler devotion

A practical guide to praying the Jesus Prayer

The young man on the bus seemed particularly cheerful. I noticed that he was clutching a woollen sort of rosary. We were on a pilgrimage in Jordan, and Johann and I were fellow passengers with Christians of different denominations. We visited a number of biblical sites but there was also space to meet one another and learn more about how we kept close to Christ. Johann's faith journey had been from Swedish Lutheran to Syrian Orthodox and, in the course of that journey, he had learned to say the Jesus Prayer. Over the week of our pilgrimage, I learned something from him of how purposeful repetition of the prayer could bring us to ride on God's waves of love, to attain more of the momentum of the Holy Spirit.

I learned that using a prayer rope could be a reminder to stick at prayer at all times. It became clear to me that Johann's enthusiasm for the Lord was nourished by his commitment to pray unceasingly, and I had never met anyone so young who had accepted that invitation from Jesus. Our common desire to build our lives on the faith of the church through the ages led to an openness between us, in which my own rather cerebral insights were exchanged for his practical hints about praying the Jesus Prayer. I was to end up building on these hints later, during the sabbatical in Guyana that I mentioned in Chapter 3.

Saying the Jesus Prayer is relatively simple, but getting into saying it was, in my own experience, a much delayed and roundabout matter, which Johann helped to determine as my unofficial spiritual guide. The external sign of the prayer rope was part of this for me, so my purchase of one on that pilgrimage was my crossing of the Rubicon, of committing myself to this discipline of prayer.

I had been used to praying with rosaries before, but they had beads that rattled. The prayer rope was different: it had but one prayer to say, woollen knot by woollen knot, and this prayer was not 'Our Father', 'Hail Mary' or 'Glory be' but one repeated sentence: 'Lord Jesus Christ, Son of God, have mercy on me, a sinner.'

You do not need a rope to say the Jesus Prayer, but it can be helpful to get hold of one to use as a prompt, since this prayer can engage body, mind and spirit. In my case, having the Jesus Prayer rope in my pocket these last seven years has marked a turning point in my Christian discipleship, for which Johann was a spur.

Comparing notes with Johann, I established that the Jesus Prayer was unlike other devotions, which could be taken and left at will. This devotional practice was an invitation from the active faith and prayer of the church through the ages to leave a lot more of myself behind and to seek God more seriously. I recognised that it came down to the way I was living my life. I celebrated and attended the Eucharist, said the daily prayers obligatory for a priest, interceded, went on pilgrimage and so on... but! That 'but' was about lack of cohesion and integration, and it reflected a failure to make Jesus Lord of my life and 'take every thought captive to obey Christ' (2 Corinthians 10:5b). There was an awful lot of John Twisleton in the gaps between my worship and prayer. Was I up to addressing this afresh, using the Jesus Prayer?

I felt I was. I felt that God wanted me to get more into a battle for my mind, as I described in Chapter 4. This meant, for example, moving from my mechanical use of the rosary, to work my mind round to a new form of repetition that is far from mechanical. To start off with, I found it hard work to get into the continuous repetition. Since the Jesus Prayer centres on addressing Jesus directly, it is hard just to rattle off the prayer to yourself. Its very nature calls forth attention and reverence.

During my Guyana sabbatical, I had plenty of time on my own, and this time became something of a battleground for my mind, emptying it of useless thoughts and filling it with the Jesus Prayer. I began to feel as if I was in a real school of contemplation, attending to the present moment through repetition of the Jesus Prayer and loosening, where possible, the grip on my mind of random thoughts, past regrets and anxieties about the future.

It is time to move from my particular faith journey to providing practical advice on saying the Jesus Prayer, gathered from different sources, so that you will be better equipped to dive in, if and when you are called to do so. In many ways, I have been privileged through my training as a priest (which is, of course, ongoing) to engage and draw on wisdom from right across the Christian tradition. I had good second-hand knowledge of the Jesus Prayer before I was led to use it, just as I had second-hand knowledge of praying in tongues before it became my own experience. One of the values of reading a book like this, on what could be called a 'speciality' of Christian spirituality, is that you are prepared for a future time in your life when that form of prayer might be energised to become a vital instrument in keeping you close to God and his heart for the world.

I don't think I would be writing this book, though, if I saw the Jesus Prayer as just a 'speciality'. It has the universal claim of Jesus about it, for is there another summary of faith that is so clear, memorable and portable? Can we find a biblical aid to praying at all times that can rival it, or any means of Holy Spirit empowerment that can so help to bypass a distracted mind? Is there an instrument of Jesus Christ anything like it for carrying his worship into life and vice versa? Like me, you may well come to invest yourself in the Jesus Prayer of Orthodoxy on account of its being a biblical aid, carried down to us by the faith of the church through the centuries. It stands unique as the gift that it is, though (as was my first impression); and, as you will shortly see, it is an appreciable and demanding task.

HOW DO YOU SAY THE JESUS PRAYER?

The first necessary clarification is that this prayer is said in both formal and free settings, which is part of its very power. Simple, memorable and short, it is a form of words that can be made part of a formal devotional time, while being offered in freer fashion as we get on with life outside set prayer times.

This is how I prayed the Jesus Prayer formally this morning. I have an oratory or prayer room in my Rectory, where I spend the first hour of the day. Half of that time I use for reciting the Jesus Prayer, and in the other half I say liturgical

Morning Prayer, which includes psalms and scripture readings, and I make intercession for my family, for my parish and for the world. To provide a framework for saying the Jesus Prayer formally, I use John Main's 'Christian meditation' pattern.[40] This involves a short spiritual reading, then getting up to stretch myself before sitting on an upright chair for an opening prayer, which moves into 30 minutes of meditation played in and out with Margaret Rizza's *Music into Silence* CD.[41]

The Benedictine monk John Main connects this pattern with the Eastern tradition of the repeated mantra mentioned in Chapter 4. Christian use of a word or phrase in prayer goes back to John Cassian (c.360–435), who popularised the wisdom of early Egyptian monasticism, and is mentioned in the medieval spiritual classic *The Cloud of Unknowing*. Main recommends the use of *Maranatha* (the Aramaic for 'Our Lord, come') as his short phrase—the short prayer used by Paul to end one of his letters (1 Corinthians 16:22). It is possible to engage with one of the global Christian Meditation groups established in line with Main's teaching, while retaining the Jesus Prayer as your prayer phrase and using a prayer rope as you meditate.[42]

Another way I pray the Jesus Prayer formally, in penitential seasons such as Advent and Lent, is to prostrate myself repeatedly. The pattern works as follows: 'Lord Jesus Christ' (touch forehead), 'Son of God' (touch the ground), 'have mercy on me, a sinner' (arise while crossing myself). Sometimes I prostrate, sometimes I stand, sometimes sit and sometimes kneel, especially before the reserved sacrament (consecrated bread kept to serve devotion), but always I repeat the traditional form of the prayer under my breath for half an hour at the start of the day. When seated, I tend to breathe in for 'Lord Jesus Christ, Son of God' and breathe out for 'have mercy on me, a sinner', which means saying ten prayers a minute, or 300 over the half-hour prayer time.

On posture, there are conflicting recommendations—sit, stand or kneel—but for the formal setting the advice from the Orthodox Church is to dispel all mental images and stand with eyes closed to focus upon the Lord. Practitioners in the West vary over the idea of praying with eyes closed. Bishop Kallistos qualifies traditional advice as he writes:

> *When you first embark on the Jesus Prayer, do not worry too much about expelling thoughts and mental pictures... let your strategy be positive, not negative. Call to mind, not what is to be excluded, but what is to be included. Do not think about your thoughts and how to shed them; think about Jesus.*[43]

It makes sense that prayer should be neither gabbled nor offered in too intense a manner. To help focus the body's engagement in the exercise, prayer ropes with 25, 50 or 100 woollen beads are available.[44] Kept in a pocket, these are also good reminders to engage in the free use of the prayer during the day.

There are variations in the form of the prayer. In his book *The Jesus Prayer*, Bishop Simon Barrington-Ward commends the traditional formula used in this book, while weighing the virtues of omitting the last few words.

> *For me, the prayer has always ended with the words, 'Lord Jesus Christ, Son of God', not with 'have mercy on me'. He is enough. He is all... the prayer springs out of this deep confidence in being loved and accepted... we are asking to become more and more ourself and to lose the false little ego which is distracting us and*

undermining us… Some prefer to drop the words 'a sinner' from the prayer, because of their association with the false guilt that the Christian Church has sometimes imposed on us. But some would want to pray the full prayer, 'have mercy on me, a sinner', just reminding ourselves of the reality that it is this sinful world, and my sinful being, which is being transformed.[45]

Another typical variation is to change the prayer into the plural: 'have mercy on us'. This broadening of the prayer is understandable, but I would defend the traditional form. The prayer is addressed to Jesus, who 'sustains all things by his powerful word' (Hebrews 1:3b), so it always brings with it the aspirations of the whole world. As Bishop Simon affirms, 'The Jesus Prayer is a participation in the movement of the redemptive love flowing through all things.'[46]

In a recent booklet, Bruce Batstone describes how he says the Jesus Prayer in his set prayer time.

To pray the prayer I find that it is best to sit or kneel in a place where you are comfortable and try to relax. Focus your attention on your breathing, and as you breathe in say the words, 'Jesus Christ, Son of God' and as you breathe out, 'have mercy on me, a sinner'. Do this gently and you will find that your breathing will slow. If you use a rope, touch a knot as you say each prayer.

Batstone addresses how best to deal with distracting thoughts, recommending that you attach your mind to the words you are repeating in prayer and recall your physical grasp of the prayer rope. He also makes it clear that 'these words are more than a mantra, they are an evocation of the name of Jesus and he is present with us as we pray'.[47]

PRAYING AT ALL TIMES

'Rejoice always,' Paul says to the Thessalonians, 'pray without ceasing, give thanks in all circumstances; for this is the will of God in Christ Jesus for you' (1 Thessalonians 5:16–18). The Jesus Prayer is a proven servant of building such a positive and prayerful attitude, by which we can rise above the heaviness of our human condition into the joy of the Lord.

Any initial conflict experienced in establishing the prayer is rewarded by the way it seems to bring something of its own momentum, moving from our hearts. In this respect, praying the Jesus Prayer without ceasing resembles praying in tongues. Both can be switched on or off, or, rather, invited by the will to fill our consciousness. Those who have experienced release of or baptism in the Holy Spirit will find that the Jesus Prayer, once established by a discipline of months and years, exercises a similar dynamic.

The other week, my wife Anne and I attended a joint New Wine and Fresh Streams leaders' meeting in Worthing, where everyone present exercised ministries that had been touched by the charismatic movement. The Canadian speaker touched on his own recent exploration of Orthodoxy through a monastic retreat and how the Jesus Prayer had been given to him by God. This opened up a fascinating discussion in which a significant number of evangelical leaders admitted that they aspired to the teaching in 1 Thessalonians to pray at all times by using both tongues and the Jesus Prayer.

Both prayer forms seem to be 'gifted' but they are started and stopped by the human will—always key to prayer. Tongues, however, operates as an unintelligible, evidently supernatural flow, in contrast to the intelligibility of the

Jesus Prayer. One of the misunderstandings about speaking in tongues is that it is beyond the control of the mind, and I needed to see through this false perception before my own initial welcoming of the gift. Similarly, the use of the Jesus Prayer is served by the conscious mind, so, even if the sense of gift is there, it always needs to be accompanied by the will to pray.

There are no short cuts when it comes to prayer. As we go about our lives 'giving thanks in all circumstances', we find that both prayer in the Spirit and the repeated flow of the Jesus Prayer are spiritual gifts aiding the accomplishment of 'the will of God in Christ Jesus for us'. That will engages with our own wills 'in all circumstances'.

At the hospital this week for an unpleasant precautionary exploration, I found myself carried along by the Jesus Prayer, so the long waiting time became a circumstance met with gratitude, which overcame my natural sense of foreboding. I found myself laying aside negative thinking, allowing a release of the inner flow of the Jesus Prayer, which I saw carrying me forward in this minor trial, keeping me courteous to those dealing with me. More than that, I became very much aware of the patients queuing with me as a spiritual responsibility and occupied myself with enfolding them in the love of Jesus. Although the Jesus Prayer continues 'have mercy on *me*, a sinner', I saw Jesus in my mind's eye holding those around me with his perfect love to cast out their fear.

The free use of the Jesus Prayer involves prayerfully tackling thoughts other than gratitude for all that comes our way. It is linked to a gladness of heart that flows from surrendering my own agenda in every circumstance, as far as I can achieve that. Thoughts come and go, allied to life's circumstances, and, since our thoughts largely determine our lives, it is a blessing to have a means of keeping Jesus in mind. The Jesus Prayer in your mind, like a WWJD bracelet on your wrist, keeps before your every circumstance that key question: 'What would Jesus do?'

Back in the village on my daily round, I feel the same inner dynamic as I stand by people: the farmer frustrated by the weather; the woman with so much to say, it's hard to get a word in; the sullen youth; the burdened church officer; the lonely old lady. All of these I engage with, while trying to let the Jesus Prayer run in me and not my own thoughts, so that any words I utter will have the Lord's weight. The prayer is nothing magical. It requires my active cooperation both to pray it in my circumstances and to let it guide my counsel.

As I write, it strikes me that the Jesus Prayer looks to be an all-encompassing devotion, although I can't claim that I have either encompassed or been encompassed by it sufficiently. At least I have got somewhat into the habit of saying sorry if I forget, for long stretches of time, to pray as I have intended. One sign that I have been forgetful is when I find myself agitated by things around me, since gladness of heart seems inseparable from surrendering oneself to God's will in every circumstance, and lack of such surrender, and of the Jesus Prayer, seems to fit the times when I feel a loss of joy.

I find that the free use of the Jesus Prayer in daily circumstances links in both with prayer in the Spirit and with liturgical prayer. At times when I am repeating the prayer, I find myself focusing on Jesus and seeing the Holy Spirit descending upon him, as at his baptism, and on those around me—as well as, at other times, inviting Jesus' own submission to the Spirit to be mine or to come into my circumstances. Another helpful connection is in using the Jesus Prayer to build on and extend my last act of Holy Communion within me and around me. Yet another aspect, linked again to my eucharistic devotion, is to see the Jesus Prayer in my daily life as recalling Jesus' offering to the Father at the Eucharist. I see myself, there and then, alongside Jesus' all-powerful offering in heaven as 'great priest over the house of God', showing forth in love his death on Calvary (Hebrews 10:21).

A SIMPLER DEVOTION

'Lord Jesus Christ, Son of God, have mercy on me, a sinner.' As we have seen, the discipline of repeating this prayer is part of 'taking every thought captive to obey Christ' (2 Corinthians 10:5).

Late evening meetings go with the territory of a commuter village. Last night's church meeting (not typical, I hasten to add!) left me with a lot of troublesome thoughts to capture. They ranged from resentment at being literally kept up by church business to exasperation about time wasted in circuitous argument and ire at a degree of discourtesy. This morning began when I awoke in the early hours, mulling over the meeting. As the thoughts I've mentioned whirred in my mind, I found my will stirring into them a repetition of the Jesus Prayer, and that is the last I remember before I woke up properly. My prayer hour proved especially valuable in settling mind and spirit, turning me away from useless mental and spiritual preoccupation with the night before.

In all the complexity of my life and work, the Jesus Prayer retains a unique capacity to centre me and bring me into the 'here and now' newness of the person of Jesus, who is 'the same yesterday and today and for ever' (Hebrews 13:8). Whatever happened last night, I can welcome his mercy and pray it for others, and this frees me to live more fully in the present moment. Past regrets have their place—the next such meeting will see me better prepared—but they are not entitled to sour my spirit. The holy name of Jesus acts in my consciousness to free me from useless preoccupation with that 'mental construct' which is the past.

As I write, I am aware that my formal use of the Jesus Prayer in the first hour of the day effects something of a cleansing of my psyche. It sets me going for continuous use of the prayer and, as a tithe of my day time, puts my later hours more fully in the Lord's hands. When I fail to commit to that early prayer, I seem set up later to confuse what is most important for me with what is merely pressing upon me as urgent.

The future is, like the past, a mental construct that besieges our spirit in the form of anxiety. Of course, I am bound to be concerned about how best to provide for things ahead of me, my family or the work of my church, but Jesus makes clear in the Gospels that those who follow him are to live without anxiety. Repeating the Jesus Prayer brings me into his joyful freedom, which exists hour by hour and refuses to be locked down by useless fears.

If the Jesus Prayer is a simpler devotion, that is mainly because it is a simple spiritual weapon. Repeating the Saviour's name is military action against the assaults of the devil that are found in wrong thinking. Each phrase of Paul's description of arming for spiritual battle seems to fit what happens as we repeat the Jesus Prayer.

> *Be strong in the Lord and in the strength of his power. Put on the whole armour of God, so that you may be able to stand against the wiles of the devil… Stand therefore, and fasten the belt of truth around your waist, and put on the breastplate of*

righteousness. As shoes for your feet put on whatever will make you ready to proclaim the gospel of peace. With all of these, take the shield of faith, with which you will be able to quench all the flaming arrows of the evil one. Take the helmet of salvation, and the sword of the Spirit, which is the word of God. **(Ephesians 6:10–11, 14–17)**

To repeat the Jesus Prayer is simple. Memorising it is no problem at all as a sentence containing the gospel and the power of the gospel. All that is required, as in any prayer, is the will to pray. Whatever is written about prayer in this book or any spiritual book fades into insignificance compared with praying itself, just as advice about weaponry is no substitute for entering the battle yourself.

CHAPTER 7

A simpler life

The joy of a centred, simplified life

We are made by our decisions.

Those who are married can look back to a time when their life was shared with a good number of friends, and how life got changed by vows of commitment to one friend as spouse. One person looms higher than any other, helping to centre, simplify and energise life through sexual union and the gift of children.

In the same way, when we find commitment to God in Jesus Christ, life is made new as we get centred and energised. Other creeds and philosophies recede in our thinking, even if we recognise their overlapping with Christianity. Through the choice of Christ as Saviour and Lord, we gain purpose for living that extends beyond this world to connect with a cause that we know is going to outlast us and, indeed, the entire universe.

Both processes are alien to many people in our Western culture who may have an exaggerated reluctance to commit, be it to marriage or religion or anything else. This is symbolised to me on the occasions when Anne and I scroll through the myriad satellite TV channels to find relaxation at the end of a tiring day, only to decide that there's no viewing worth the choice. Life nowadays can so often feel like jumping between seemingly fruitless options.

Even the life of believers can lack fruitfulness on account of this sort of consumerist stroll round the spiritual marketplace, 'looking for a thrill'. This happens despite our being called by Jesus to live as citizens building God's kingdom rather than consumers foraging for spiritual benefits.

I am not suggesting that the variety of Christian disciplines available is anything amiss. As I reflect on my faith pilgrimage, I see how it has drawn on means of grace that are biblical (evangelical), sacramental (catholic), charismatic (pentecostal) and from the world (liberal/radical) in the sense of engaging with God beyond church walls. I have found myself drawn to Jesus through word and sacrament, through Holy Spirit empowerment and within the world he made, loves and indwells.

The Jesus Prayer has woven itself through me, around me and into me, so that I cannot but witness to it as a timely device from the Lord that centres, simplifies and energises his disciples. There is a sense in me that I did not choose this form of prayer but that it chose me, and did so as part of the Lord's call for me to work towards a life of unceasing prayer.

I cannot be the ultimate judge, but the decision to accept God's invitation, given through prayer, people and circumstances, to use the Jesus Prayer seems to have indeed centred and so simplified and energised my life—not just my spiritual life but the whole show, so to speak. In that it keeps me aware of the Lord between the occasions of formal prayer and worship, there is a counter to the loss of moral and spiritual intention. Just as God is the still point at the centre of all things, repetition of the holy name of Jesus is a grace that holds me to that centre, 'a sure and steadfast anchor of the soul, a hope that enters the inner shrine behind the curtain, where Jesus, a forerunner on our behalf, has entered' (Hebrews 6:19–20).

You can, of course, be decided and centred on God in Christ without using the Jesus Prayer. In writing this book, I am speaking from my individual faith pilgrimage, which I hope shows a breadth of Christian sympathy. Within that breadth, I have often come close to losing my focus, so that in taking or leaving devotional practices, I have ended up doing more of what *I* wanted in dropping disciplines that chafed me. I cannot guarantee I won't drop the Jesus Prayer, despite having written at such length about it, but, if I were to attempt to do so, I feel I would be discouraged from taking a final decision by the thought of losing the precious simplicity it has provided for me over the last seven years of my life. I am aware of so much evidence that self has lost ground and Christ has gained ground in my life through use of the prayer, and that something of the freedom of God's children has been taking root in me as I've expressed through it an ongoing decision for him.

THE WHOLE CHRIST

Thoroughly biblical, carried forward by the faith of the church through the centuries, the Jesus Prayer stands as a unique gift and task. Its attractiveness lies in the way it states simple Christianity and seems to carry within it the momentum of the Spirit, as well as the way it serves believers struggling to integrate minds and hearts, so that their will can be enfolded by that of Jesus Christ.

In suggesting that the Jesus Prayer has the momentum of the Spirit, I am thinking of Paul's advice that 'no one can say "Jesus is Lord" except by the Holy Spirit' (1 Corinthians 12:3b). It is the Spirit working in the Church who excites the proclamation of Jesus as Lord, and so the spread of the Jesus Prayer is surely from that source. By the Spirit, the risen Lord Jesus builds up his body, since all who profess Jesus are made one with him. To pray the Jesus Prayer is to be made one with Jesus' prayer and to grow with all things 'to the unity of the faith and of the knowledge of the Son of God, to maturity, to the measure of the full stature of Christ' (Ephesians 4:13).

Another evidence for the momentum of the Spirit is my experience, and that of others, of seeing how the discipline of repetition is accompanied by many occasions when the prayer keeps going even when, as in sleep, the human will to pray has failed. Like the Holy Spirit, who prays within believers, it could be said of the Jesus Prayer that it 'helps us in our weakness; for we do not know how to pray as we ought' (Romans 8:26).

All prayer is through, with and in Jesus Christ, Son of God and the world's merciful Saviour. Praying the Jesus Prayer is about being caught up with all things, as well as yourself lifting up all things, into God's merciful love. Just as, in the Eucharist, we offer Christ's sacrifice as well as our own, since our life is hidden in him (Colossians 3:3b), when we pray the Jesus Prayer it is the whole Christ, head and members, offering the whole Christ for the glory of God and the transformation of the universe.

Christ is not some extra feature added to the world, an embellishment, a king such as we crown, the owner of a great estate… he is the Alpha and the Omega, the principle and the end, the foundation stone and the keystone, the plenitude… he is the one who consummates and the one who gives consistence to all things. To him and through him, the interior life and light of the world is effected, in pain and labour, the universal convergence of all created spirit. He is the one single centre, precious and stable, that shines out at the summit, still to come, of the world, in diametric opposition to the dim and eternally shrinking regions into which our science ventures when it travels down the road of matter and the past.[48]

In these words, Teilhard de Chardin affirms the future orientation of Christianity through Jesus 'in whom all things [will] hold together' (Colossians 1:17b) over against the tendency of science to reduce the mystery of the ongoing creation. To pray in the name of Jesus is therefore to invoke the first-born and head of all things, in whom and through whom all things have been launched, hold together and are consummated.

Prayer and Eucharist, individual and Christian community, locality and cosmos, will and Holy Spirit inspiration, past and future—all find a centre in the discipline and gift of the Jesus Prayer.

TO PRAY WITHOUT CEASING

On the 24th Sunday after Pentecost I went to church to say my prayers there during the Liturgy. The first Epistle of St Paul to the Thessalonians was being read, and among other words I heard these—'Pray without ceasing'. It was this text, more than any other, which forced itself upon my mind, and I began to think how it was possible to pray without ceasing, since a man has to concern himself with other things also in order to make a living... 'What ought I to do?' I thought. 'Where shall I find someone to explain it to me?'[49]

This is how the pilgrim starts his story in the Russian spiritual classic *The Way of a Pilgrim* and his question of how it is possible to 'pray without ceasing' lies behind the gift and task of the Jesus Prayer that I have been addressing in this book.

In *The Way of a Pilgrim* we read how the pilgrim goes first to 'a gentleman who had long been living and seeking the salvation of his soul'.

He was silent for a while and looked at me closely. Then he said: 'Ceaseless interior prayer is a continual yearning of the human spirit towards God. To succeed in this consoling exercise we must pray more often to God to teach us to pray without ceasing. Pray more, and pray more fervently. It is prayer itself which will reveal to you how it can be achieved unceasingly; but it will take some time.'

In the narrative, the pilgrim continues on his journey, asking the same question of various holy people. I mentioned earlier how he finally gets the advice which is being repeated in this book, namely to adopt 'the continuous interior Prayer of Jesus... a constant uninterrupted calling upon the divine Name of Jesus with the lips, in the spirit, in the heart; while forming a mental picture of His constant presence'.[50]

Through his call to pray unceasingly, and the advice he receives, the pilgrim sets himself to repeat the Jesus Prayer continuously. It is unclear whether the account is from the experiences of an actual pilgrim or whether the book is a fiction to teach about ceaseless prayer and communion with God. Either way, the reader is drawn into the subject's enthusiastic venture towards ceaseless prayer as the goal of life or, really, 'life itself', and follows how the acceptance of the task of repeating the Jesus Prayer is blessed by the Holy Spirit. This task is effected under the authority of spiritual guides, building on the writings in *The Philokalia* and with the pilgrim's full involvement in the worship and discipline of the church. The discipline to which he submits opens his perception marvellously so that he comes to see the natural world around him as being woven into his prayer:

> *With the help [*The Philiokalia*] gave me I began to some extent to understand the hidden meaning of the word of God. I began to see the meaning of such sayings as—'The inner secret man of the heart', 'true prayer worships in the spirit', 'the kingdom of God is within us', 'the intercession of the Holy Spirit with groaning that cannot be uttered', 'abide in me', 'the betrothal of the Spirit to our hearts', the cry from the depths of the heart, 'Abba, Father' and so on. And when with all this in mind I prayed with my heart, everything around me seemed delightful and marvellous. The trees, the grass, the birds, the earth, the air, the light seemed to be telling me that they existed for man's sake, that they witnessed to the love of God for man, that everything proved the love of God for man, that all things prayed to God and sang His praise.*[51]

This mystical description indicates the fruit of his pilgrimage—how the Spirit carries him forward so as to open the eye of his mind and heart to a far bigger and more exciting vision of the meaning and significance of creation. All of this comes from accepting that word from the Lord in the first letter of

Paul to the Thessalonians—'pray without ceasing'—and the practical aid of the Jesus Prayer as servant of this task.

A SIMPLER LIFE

Our youngest son left home for university this week, so the house has rather an empty feel about it. It is one of those lesser bereavements in life, which ultimately makes space for everyone in different ways. Through Skype, James has just made himself present to us again and given us a tour of his room and a quick show on-screen of his new friends. He has gone from us but is still with us, since we have a means of coming close to him through Skype, alongside other means of communication.

Is it fanciful to see the electronic realm that brought our son almost literally before us as an analogy of the spiritual realm through which God brings himself before us? Could we say that prayer is akin to Skyping? The presence of God may be more certainly before us in the blessed sacrament than in the Jesus Prayer, but, like Holy Communion, 'invocation of the divine name possesses a sacramental character, serving as an efficacious sign of his invisible presence and action'.[52] The word 'efficacious' means 'being capable of producing the desired effect', in this case a sense of the consoling presence of Jesus. Since James left, the sense of his absence has been woven into my prayer, which, centred on Jesus, brings with it the assurance of our continuing as one, although in a new way.

'Lord Jesus Christ, Son of God, have mercy on me, a sinner': the Lord Jesus is the perfect expression of God's love, who, as both God and a human being, can fully sympathise with our sorrows and joys. Though life in this world is fragmented and fragmentary, the wholeness of Christ draws us into himself so that our hurts are consoled and our joys shared. In the Jesus Prayer we are given grace to counter the gravitational downward pull of sorrow and sin, so as to achieve lightness of spirit. The struggle with relationships and insecurities and even faith pulls us down, as into quicksand, but as Christians we can welcome the upward pull of Jesus, which lifts us when we are down. In repeating the Jesus Prayer, we put faith in God who is rich in mercy and we see how 'efficacious' that mercy is as it responds to heartfelt prayer.

'God loves me! What joy! And I truly love him too!' is a paraphrase of the Jesus Prayer—a simple sentence declaring simple yet awesome truth. As the prayer continues within me, it establishes faith in God's love for me and for all that is, minute by minute, day by day and for all eternity. It announces Jesus who came and died long ago to be my living Lord and Saviour this day, by whose mercy I exist and by trust in whose mercy I can fully prosper. Jesus, who came to bring life and bring it to the full, is placed before me by the act of faith expressed in this prayer. It is a touching of the Lord who fills my hour-by-hour inner emptiness as I reach up to him. There is no more precious knowledge on earth than that you are loved immensely, and will be so loved for all eternity.

How is it that our awareness of this saving knowledge comes and goes? It is because we are mere creatures, and creatures can't get their minds fully round the one who created them, for if they could, they too would be God. The secret of the Christian life is actually simple: to so live in God's love as to be its channel. Like all simple things, we disbelieve it and complicate it, and sometimes run away from it, but the truth about Jesus isn't changed by our failure to grasp it. Our best resources, found through the church, are the reminders of God in Christ that we have celebrated in this book—scripture and sacrament, prayer and the fellowship and guidance of other Christians. Inasmuch as the Jesus Prayer acts as a reminder of God's love, it is to be commended as the gift and task it is, with its capacity to generate unceasing prayer.

To admit continuously that I am a sinner in need of God's mercy in Jesus Christ places me in fellowship with saints of old who professed not just their sinfulness but their being 'the worst' of sinners (1 Timothy 1:15b, NIV). It is the simplest place to put myself, at the foot of the cross. When I read the lives of Christians adorned with heroic virtues who acknowledged that they were 'the worst of sinners', I used to struggle to understand. Saying the phrase 'have mercy on me, a sinner' in the Jesus Prayer sounded like false modesty. It might be the prayer of the tax collector and not the Pharisee (Luke 18:9–14) but its constant repetition sounded to me dangerously Pharisaical! What wins me to even deeper ownership of the Jesus Prayer is the increasing awareness of my state before God as one who is really and truly much in need of his mercy.

I was standing the other day in Westminster Abbey before the high altar where, for half the Christian era, English monarchs have been anointed within the Eucharist. Over that altar, these aspirational words are inscribed from Revelation 11:15: 'The kingdom of this world is become the kingdom of our God and of his Christ.'

As I looked around the abbey at the memorials of the famous, I wondered how many of them were so excited by Jesus Christ and struck by his merciful provision that they took that aspiration with them to the splendour of their tombs. My visit coincided with the installation of a memorial to poet and Christian apologist C.S. Lewis, which has these words of his inscribed upon it: 'I believe in Christianity as I believe that the Sun has risen, not only because I see it but because by it I see everything else.'

May God raise up women and men with that vision, who see 'the light of the knowledge of the glory of God in the face of Jesus Christ' (2 Corinthians 4:6b), and may the gift of the Jesus Prayer serve that end! If the future of the world depends on the mission of Jesus Christ given to his Church, the loss of passion among church members to work for 'the kingdom of this world' to 'become the kingdom of our God and of his Christ' (Revelation 11:15) should be our gravest concern. This loss of energy is the product of many influences but one factor is the failure of contemporary Christianity to provide simple, clear and effective means of discipleship. There is plentiful evidence of the outpouring of the Holy Spirit over the last century, which has brought three of the sundered branches of the church—Catholic, Protestant and Pentecostal—into new dialogue. The more recent entry of Eastern Orthodox Christianity into this dialogue has brought with it new riches, including centuries-old wisdom about the use of the Jesus Prayer. May my experience be that of many others in welcoming the Lord's invitation to use this prayer, find a simpler Christian life and gain fresh energy for the work of establishing God's kingdom.

Afterword

So is the Jesus Prayer for you, or is it something you're grateful to know about, for which you will await God's call?

My own catholic-evangelical theological inclination, coupled with my need to find a way to cool my mind for prayer, got me interested. These two factors gave me fertile ground to receive the invitation of the Holy Spirit to start the Jesus Prayer when that invitation came through holy people I met at a propitious time in my life.

Space must be the key—and do not think continuous repetition of 'Lord Jesus Christ, Son of God, have mercy on me' will cut space from your life. The Jesus Prayer is like a narrow door, but once you pass through and into its use, you will find plenty of space.

To follow up this book, why not get hold of a copy of *The Way of a Pilgrim* and read the compelling tale of the Russian pilgrim in quest of ceaseless prayer? If you want a shorter practical guide on the Jesus Prayer, I would commend Bishop Kallistos Ware's booklet *The Power of the Name*.

To have memorised this simple one-line prayer will at least be useful when sleep fails you. Its slow repetition is the best antidote to small hours' insomnia I've ever found.

Pray as you can, not as you can't. The world is being changed by your prayer, and the more heart you can put into it, however it is expressed, the better for the world.

Notes

1 E. Kadloubovsky and G.E.H. Palmer (trans.), *Writings from the Philokalia on Prayer of the Heart* (Faber & Faber, 1977), p. 319.
2 Abbé de Tourville, *Letters of Direction* (Dacre Press, 1939), p. 83.
3 Bishop Kallistos of Diokleia, *The Power of the Name* (SLG, 2007), pp. 6–7.
4 John Twisleton, *Meet Jesus* (BRF, 2011), pp. 40–44.
5 Kadloubovsky and Palmer, *Writings from the Philokalia.*
6 Words of administration at Holy Communion, Book of Common Prayer (1662).
7 'O God, unseen yet ever near' by E. Osler, *Hymns Ancient & Modern Revised,* No. 412.
8 *Common Worship: Daily Prayer* (Church House Publishing, 2005), pp. 252–253.
9 Abbé de Tourville, *Letters of Direction,* p. 78.
10 Kadloubovsky and Palmer, *Writings from the Philokalia,* p. 225.
11 Bishop Kallistos, *Power of the Name,* p. 18.
12 W.E. Vine, *Expository Dictionary of Bible Words* Vol III (Marshall, Morgan & Scott, 1981), p. 61.
13 Vine, *Expository Dictionary of Bible Words,* p. 62.
14 Philip Yancey, *What's So Amazing About Grace?* (Zondervan, 1997), p. 271.
15 Donald Coggan, *Cuthbert Bardsley* (Collins, 1989), pp. 154–160.
16 Simon Barrington-Ward, *The Jesus Prayer* (BRF, 2007), p. 93.
17 Kadloubovsky and Palmer, *Writings from the Philokalia.*
18 Kadloubovsky and Palmer, *Writings from the Philokalia,* p. 303.
19 Kadloubovsky and Palmer, *Writings from the Philokalia,* pp. 291–292.
20 R.M. French (trans.), *The Way of a Pilgrim* (SPCK, 1965).
21 French, *Way of a Pilgrim,* pp. 8–10.
22 Sergius Bulgakov, quoted by Timothy Ware, *The Orthodox Church* (Penguin, 1967), p. 313.
23 French, *Way of a Pilgrim,* p. 134.

24 Bishop Kallistos, *Power of the Name*, pp. 5, 10.
25 Kadloubovsky and Palmer, *Writings from the Philokalia*, pp. 307–308.
26 Christopher C.H. Cook, *The Philokalia and the Inner Life* (James Clarke, 2011).
27 A.C. Spearing (trans.), *The Cloud of Unknowing and Other Works* (Penguin Classics, 2001).
28 Kadloubovsky and Palmer, *Writings from the Philokalia*, p. 228.
29 Ana Smiljanic (trans.), *Our Thoughts Determine Our Lives: The life and teaching of Elder Thaddeus of Vitovnica* (Saint Herman of Alaska Brotherhood, 2012), p. 110.
30 Smiljanic, *Our Thoughts Determine Our Lives*, pp. 111–112.
31 Anthony De Mello SJ, *Sadhana—A Way to God: Christian exercises in eastern form* (Image Books, 1978), p. 115.
32 Barrington-Ward, *The Jesus Prayer*, p. 25.
33 Smiljanic, *Our Thoughts Determine Our Lives*, p. 114–115.
34 'Directions to hesychasts by the monks Callistus and Ignatius of Xanthopoulos', in Kadloubovsky and Palmer, *Writings from the Philokalia*, p. 259.
35 Kadloubovsky and Palmer, *Writings from the Philokalia*, p. 264.
36 The Bishops of England and Wales, *Celebrating the Mass* (2005), p. 54.
37 A Monk of the Eastern Church, *On the Invocation of the Name of Jesus* (Fellowship of St Alban and St Sergius, 1949), p. 19.
38 T.F. Torrance, in *Theology in Reconciliation* (Geoffrey Chapman, 1975), pp. 132–134, quoted in Rowan Williams *Eucharistic Sacrifice: The roots of a metaphor* (Grove, 1982), p. 33.
39 Bishop Kallistos, *Power of the Name*, p. 13.
40 John Main, *Word into Silence* (Canterbury, 2006).
41 Margaret Rizza, *Music into Silence* CD (Medio Media, www.wccm.org).
42 The World Community for Christian Meditation (www.wccm.org).
43 Bishop Kallistos, *Power of the Name*, p. 18.
44 Crawley Down Monastery, Crawley Down, Crawley RH10 4LH.

45 Barrington-Ward, *Jesus Prayer*, pp. 87–88, 90.
46 Barrington-Ward, *Jesus Prayer*, p. 93.
47 Bruce Batstone, *Still Listening: Considering the Jesus Prayer* (Urbanquiet, 2011).
48 Teilhard de Chardin, Letter of 19 June 1926, quoted in Henri de Lubac, SJ, *The Religion of Teilhard de Chardin* (Collins, 1967), p. 106.
49 French, *Way of a Pilgrim*, p. 1.
50 French, *Way of a Pilgrim*, pp. 2–3, 8.
51 French, *Way of a Pilgrim*, p. 31.
52 Bishop Kallistos, *Power of the Name*, p. 13.

ALSO BY JOHN TWISLETON

Meet Jesus

A call to adventure

To engage with Jesus expands the mind and heart. It challenges our view of the way the world is, where it is heading and what difference we could make to it. But in a world of competing philosophies, where does Jesus fit in? How far can we trust the Bible and the Church? What difference does Jesus make to our lives and communities? Is Jesus really the be all and end all?

Meet Jesus is a lively and straightforward exploration of these and other questions, with the aim of engaging our reason, inspiring our faith and worship, deepening our fellowship and service, and bringing new depth to our witness to the world. Each chapter ends with some practical points for action and the book concludes with a section of discussion material for groups.

ALSO FROM BRF

The Jesus Prayer

SIMON BARRINGTON-WARD

The Jesus Prayer has been known and loved by generations of Christians. Originating in the Orthodox Church, it is a way of entering into the river of prayer that flows from the heart of God, as Jesus continually prays for his people and for the world he loves. Within us, too, the Spirit of God prays 'with sighs too deep for words', and the Jesus Prayer can help us to join in the loving intercession of God-in-Christ for the redemption of all things.

In this new edition of a BRF classic, Simon Barrington-Ward teaches us how to use the prayer, and provides biblical and historical background for understanding its significance.

ALSO FROM BRF

Creating a Life with God

The call of ancient prayer practices

DANIEL WOLPERT

Are you longing to take your relationship with God to a new level? This book introduces twelve prayer practices that

- invite you to solitude and silence
- invite you to use your mind and imagination
- invite you to use your body and your creativity
- invite you to connect with nature and community

You'll meet 'travelling companions' from history, such as Ignatius Loyola and Julian of Norwich, whose lives were illuminated by these ways of praying. An appendix offers step-by-step instructions for practising the Jesus Prayer and the prayer of examen, for walking a labyrinth, praying with your body, and more—whether individually or as a group.

ALSO FROM BRF

Discovering the Spiritual Exercises of Saint Ignatius

LARRY WARNER

This book is an adaptation of the Spiritual Exercises of St Ignatius Loyola, to help you to embark on a life-transforming journey toward Christlikeness. For nearly 500 years, the Exercises have been a tool for spiritual formation, and are now experiencing something of a revival across the breadth of the Church.

This is not a book about the methods or techniques of Christian formation but one that enables you to come before God through the Gospel narratives in order to encounter Jesus afresh. If you hunger for something deeper, yearn to walk with Jesus and desire to embrace more of what God is doing in and through you, then this is the book for you.

ALSO FROM BRF

Simple Gifts

Blessings in disguise

KEVIN SCULLY

We are familiar with the idea of friendship as a gift, something that bestows blessing on our lives. Hospitality enriches both giver and receiver, while humour is a gift that, used sensitively, can shed a warm light even on a bleak situation. There are other aspects of life that we may take for granted or even actively dislike—aspects such as ignorance, tears, grief and anger.

Drawing on scripture, song, poetry and insights from daily life, Kevin Scully considers different facets of ten such gifts, from the familiar to the unexpected. He shows how each has the potential to be a source of personal wonder and joy and can also draw us closer to God and to one another. *Simple Gifts* is a book that can be read from beginning to end or dipped into for reflection or inspiration.

ALSO FROM BRF

Moments of Grace

Reflections on meeting with God

JOY MACCORMICK

From desolation to celebration, loneliness to love, *Moments of Grace* offers pithy, thought-provoking reflections on themes connecting God, faith and the journey of life. Questions for further pondering help the reader make links between head and heart, between what they believe, what they wrestle with believing and what they experience day by day.

Joy MacCormick, a New Zealand Anglican priest, has written this book to help people have a closer encounter with God in prayer, especially those who may struggle to find a place in conventional church worship.

ALSO FROM BRF

Learning with Foundations21: Prayer

A seven-week course of study material for individuals and groups

CLAIRE MUSTERS

This study resource provides seven weeks of material for group or individual use. Each week includes an overview session with shorter follow-up sessions through the week, with questions and activities differentiated for different learning styles, and links to the Foundations21 website for those wishing to explore further.

Wk 1: What is prayer?
Wk 2: Prayer in the Bible
Wk 3: Praying Jesus' way
Wk 4: Ways in to prayer
Wk 5: The discipline of prayer
Wk 6: The power of prayer
Wk 7: Praying with others

ISBN 978 1 84101 851 5   £7.99
Available from your local Christian bookshop or direct from BRF: visit www.brfonline.org.uk

ALSO FROM BRF

Rhythms of Grace

Finding intimacy with God in a busy life

TONY HORSFALL

Rhythms of Grace emerges from a personal exploration of contemplative spirituality. Coming from an evangelical and charismatic background, Tony Horsfall felt an increasing desire to know God more deeply. At the same time, he felt an increasing dissatisfaction with his own spiritual life, as well as concern at the number of highly qualified and gifted people involved in Christian ministry who experience burn-out.

In this book he shows how contemplative spirituality, with its emphasis on realising our identity as God's beloved children and on being rather than doing, has vital lessons for us about discovering intimacy with God.